Key Resources
for
Future Teachers

Pamela J. Farris
Northern Illinois University

Boston   Burr Ridge, IL   Dubuque, IA   Madison, WI   New York   San Francisco   St. Louis
Bangkok   Bogotá   Caracas   Lisbon   London   Madrid
Mexico City   Milan   New Delhi   Seoul   Singapore   Sydney   Taipei   Toronto

McGraw-Hill Higher Education

A Division of The McGraw-Hill Companies

KEY RESOURCES FOR FUTURE TEACHERS

Published by McGraw-Hill Higher Education, an operating unit of The McGraw-Hill Companies, Inc., Dubuque, Iowa. Copyright © 2000 by The McGraw-Hill Companies, Inc. All rights reserved. Printed in the United States of America.

This book is printed on acid-free paper.

1 2 3 4 5 6 7 8 9 0 QPD QPD 9 0 3 2 1 0 9

ISBN 0-07-241597-5

www.mhhe.com

Table of Contents

Goals 2000: Educate America Act

The Goals 2000 Act Supporting Community Efforts to Reach Challenging Goals and High Standards

Since 1983, when the report "A Nation at Risk" sent alarming signals across America that our nation's public schools were not preparing our youth for the changing times, many state and local leaders have been engaged in school reform. What we have all learned from their experiences has shaped the principles underlying the Goals 2000: Educate America Act—the need for high expectations for students, full participation by parents, educators and communities in education, safe and disciplined learning environments, quality teaching and professional development, the effective use of technology in learning, long-term systemwide improvement efforts, and communities and states custom-making school improvement efforts to meet their needs.

Goals 2000 has drawn broad support from both major political parties, parents, and representatives of the business community, governors, teachers, labor, school administrators, state legislators, school boards, and state school superintendents.

The Act recognizes that there is no simple or cookie cutter approach to improving education. It supports a wide array of state and local approaches to raise academic achievement, and to provide a safe, disciplined learning environment for all children. The Goals 2000 Act "reaffirms that the responsibility for control of education is reserved to the states and local school systems."

Major Directions of Goals 2000

Improving Student Achievement—High Expectations for All

What we've learned: We've learned that children often meet expectations set for them. U.S. Education Secretary—and former South Carolina Governor—Richard Riley cites the urgent need for "ending the tyranny of low expectations" that is blocking the progress of many of our students.

What Goals 2000 helps states and communities to do: States and communities are being asked to make their own high expectations concrete by establishing standards for what children should learn and know how to do. These standards would be in core academic subjects, such as math, science and English. Voluntary national standards could be used as models for academic excellence to help set challenging learning standards.

Source: United States Department of Education.

Increasing Parent and Community Involvement in Education

What we've learned: While schools have been given an important responsibility for helping communities and parents to educate children, we have learned that schools cannot do it alone. Students simply achieve more when there is meaningful parental and community involvement in their children's education. Parents and families are often our "secret weapon" to improve student learning. The American family is the rock on which a solid education can and must be built.

What Goals 2000 helps states and communities to do: The Goals 2000 Act encourages the building of strong family-school partnerships for learning. Schools need to open their doors for parental and community involvement in the design and implementation of school improvement efforts. At the state and local level, broad-based panels will develop and oversee the implementation of improvement efforts, including strengthening parental involvement in learning.

Finally, Goals 2000 authorizes the creation of parent resource centers to support strong and effective parental involvement.

Making Schools Safe, Drug-Free, and Disciplined

What we've learned: Students learn better when they are in orderly environments in which they feel safe. Such environments also make it possible for teachers to focus on teaching and provide students with real opportunities for learning.

What Goals 2000 helps states and communities to do: States and communities can address ways to make schools safe, drug-free, and more disciplined as part of their improvement efforts. In addition, Title VII of Goals 2000, entitled the Safe Schools Act, authorizes the Secretary of Education to award competitive grants to school districts to help them reduce violence. Grants of up to $3 million each may be made for periods up to two years. These funds can support activities ranging from the installation of metal detectors to comprehensive violence prevention efforts, which might include mentoring programs and the training of school personnel in conflict resolution.

Related activities could also be supported by the crime prevention authority in the crime bill that recently passed Congress. This bill provides substantial new funds for community and school efforts to prevent and reduce violence.

Upgrading Teacher Training and Professional Development

What we've learned: Improving student achievement depends on the ability of teachers to teach challenging subject matter to all students, and to manage effectively an orderly learning environment. Prospective and current teachers need sustained and meaningful opportunities to learn how to do these things well.

What Goals 2000 helps states and communities to do: Participating states will develop competitive grant processes to award at least 60 percent of Goals 2000 funds in the first year—and at least 90 percent in subsequent years—to school districts for the development of reform plans, *and* for improving professional development opportunities for prospective and current teachers. Subgrants for professional development will be awarded by the state to school districts working with institutions of higher education and other non-profit organizations.

Bringing Technology into the Schools

What we've learned: The use of educational technologies—including computers in the classroom—can improve student achievement, support professional development, and increase the learning resources available to our students. In this information age, students must be prepared to use computers and other technology in school and beyond.

What Goals 2000 helps states and communities to do: Goals 2000 funds can be used by states to integrate technology into their school improvement efforts. It also creates an Office of Educational Technology within the Department of Education, charged with supporting state and local efforts to bring technology into the classrooms.

Supporting Long-Term and Systemwide Efforts

What we've learned: Improving schools involves intensive and long-term effort. Moreover, success depends on ensuring that all parts of an educational system are working together to help all children reach challenging academic standards. Reforms are less likely to lead to gains in student achievement when focus is placed on only one piece of an educational system, rather than on all pieces and how they fit together. A piecemeal approach, for example, might focus on professional development or educational technology without looking at challenging standards for what communities want their children to learn, or rigorous assessments of learning.

What Goals 2000 helps states and communities to do: At the heart of Goals 2000 is the grant program for the development and implementation of long-term comprehensive school improvements. Participating states and communities are being supported in their efforts to set high academic standards and goals, and improve all aspects of education to reinforce the achievement of these standards and goals—including parent involvement, the use of better assessments, professional development, technology, and how related education and training initiatives can work together to improve student achievement.

Communities, States Tailoring Improvements to Their Needs

What we've learned: Improvements in education are most likely to take place when schools, districts, and states have the flexibility and support needed to custom-make their own strategies to improve student achievement. This approach is particularly effective when new flexibility is exchanged for accountability based on results.

This lesson highlights the need for a new role of government at all levels—one that focuses on removing unnecessary barriers to improvement, and supporting those closest to the classroom and community as they work to improve their schools.

What Goals 2000 helps states and communities to do: Under Goals 2000, the focus of government shifts from rules and compliance, and toward flexibility and support for high student achievement and accountability for results. Moreover, Goals 2000 provides support for communities and state to custom-make their own improvement efforts to meet their own needs. The two-page Goals 2000 application and the absence of any regulations associated with the Goals 2000 plans are important—and unprecedented—manifestations of this new partnership.

The Goals 2000 Act provides new waiver authority to the Secretary of Education to cut through federal red tape in education. Once a state reform plan is approved, the state may ask the Secretary to waive requirements of certain federal education programs that the state has determined impede the implementation of state or local plans. State educational agencies may also submit waiver requests on behalf of local educational agencies and schools.

In addition, six states will be selected for participation in an education flexibility demonstration program. This provision authorizes the Secretary to *delegate* his waiver authority to state educational agencies.

Helping to Reach the National Education Goals

The Goals 2000 Act formalizes in law eight national education goals. These goals constitute a lighthouse that can guide the efforts of communities and states to improve education. The Goals are: By the year 2000 . . .

School readiness. All children in America will start school ready to learn.

Increased graduation rate. The high school graduation rate will increase to at least 90 percent.

Improved student achievement. All students in America will be competent in the core academic subjects.

Adult literacy and lifelong learning. Every adult American will be literate and possess the skills necessary to compete in the economy of the twenty-first century.

Teacher education and professional development. All teachers will have the opportunity to acquire the knowledge and skills needed to prepare U.S. students for the next century.

Best in math and science. U.S. students will be first in the world in math and science.

Safe, disciplined, and drug-free schools. Every school in America will be safe, disciplined, and drug-free.

Parental involvement. Every school will promote parental involvement in their children's education.

Conclusion

Together, these school improvement efforts—supported by Goals 2000—can help create a new ethic of learning in this country and play a critical role in helping children reach challenging goals and standards. These efforts can help create better education and training opportunities—geared to the needs of states and local communities—to best support children's success in school, in the workplace, and as responsible citizens in our nation's democracy.

Goals 2000: Educate America Act Supporting Communities and States to Improve Student Achievement

Overview

- The Goals 2000 Act provides resources to states and communities to develop and implement comprehensive education reforms aimed at helping students reach challenging academic and occupational skill standards.

Legislative Review

- On March 23, 1994, the House of Representatives approved the final Goals 2000 bill by a bipartisan vote of 306–121. On March 26, the Senate approved Goals 2000 by a bipartisan vote of 63–22.

- The President signed the bill into law March 31, 1994.

Timetable and Funding

- Congress appropriated $105 million for Goals 2000 for fiscal year 1994. First-year funds became available to the states on July 1, 1994. The President asked Congress for a substantial increase for fiscal year 1995. A House-Senate conference committee determines the final appropriation for Goals 2000 for each fiscal year through the year 2000.

- For first-year funding, states were asked to submit an application describing how a broad-based citizen panel would develop an action plan to improve their schools. The application also described how subgrants will be made for local education improvement and better teacher preservice and professional development programs.

- During the first year, states used at least 60 percent of their allotted funds to award subgrants to local school districts for the development or implementation of local and individual school improvement efforts, and for better teacher education programs and professional development activities.

- In succeeding years, at least 90 percent of each state's funds will be used to make subgrants for the implementation of the state, local, and individual school improvement plans and to support teacher education and professional development.
- During the first year, local districts used at least 75 percent of the funds they received to support individual school improvement initiatives. After the first year, districts passed through at least 85 percent of the funds to schools.

Components of the "Goals 2000: Educate America Act"

Title I: Setting High Expectations for Our Nation: the National Education Goals

Formalizes in law the original six National Education Goals. These goals concern: readiness for school; increased school graduation rates; student academic achievement and citizenship; mathematics and science performance; adult literacy; and safe, disciplined, and drug-free schools. The Act adds two new goals that encourage parental participation and better professional development for teachers and principals.

Title II: Public Accountability for Progress Toward the Goals and Development of Challenging, Voluntary, Academic Standards

Establishes in law the bipartisan National Education Goals Panel, which will: report on the nation's progress toward meeting the goals; build public support for taking actions to meet the goals; and review the voluntarily-submitted national standards and the criteria for certification of these standards developed by the National Education Standards and Improvement Council.

- Creates the National Education Standards and Improvement Council, made up of a bipartisan, broad base of citizens and educators, to examine and certify voluntary national and state standards submitted on a voluntary basis by states and by organizations working on particular academic subjects.
- Authorizes grants to support the development of voluntary assessment systems aligned to state standards, and for the development of *model* opportunity-to-learn standards.

Title III: Supporting Community and State Efforts to Improve Education

- The central purpose of the Goals 2000 Act is to support, accelerate, and sustain state and local improvement efforts aimed at helping students reach challenging academic and occupational standards.

Broad-Based Citizen Involvement in State Improvement Efforts

- The Governor and the Chief State School Officer will each appoint half the members of a broad-based panel. This panel will be comprised of teachers, principals, administrators, parents, representatives of business, labor, and higher education, and members of the public, as well as the chair of the state board of education and the chairs of the appropriate authorizing committees of the state legislature.
- States that already have a broad-based panel in place that has made substantial progress in developing a reform plan may request that the Secretary of Education recognize the existing panel.

Comprehensive Improvement Plan Geared to High Standards of Achievement

- The State Planning Panel is responsible for developing a comprehensive reform plan.
- States with reform plans already in place that meet the Act's requirements will not have to develop new plans for Goals 2000. The U.S. Secretary of Education may approve plans, or portions of plans, already adopted by the state.

- In order to receive Goals 2000 funds after the first year, a state has to have an approved plan or have made substantial progress in developing it.
- A peer review process will be used to review the state plans and offer guidance to the State Planning Panel. The U.S. Department of Education also will offer other technical assistance and support by drawing on the expertise of successful educators and leaders from around the nation.

In general, the plans are to address:

- Strategies for the development or adoption of content standards, student performance standards, student assessments, and plans for improving teacher training.
- Strategies to involve parents and the community in helping all students meet challenging state standards and to promote grass-roots, bottom-up involvement in reform.
- Strategies for ensuring that all local educational agencies and schools in the state are involved in developing and implementing needed improvements.
- Strategies for improved management and governance, and for promoting accountability for results, flexibility, site-based management, and other principles of high-performance management.
- Strategies for providing all students an opportunity to learn at higher academic levels.
- Strategies for assisting local educational agencies and schools to meet the needs of school-age students who have dropped out of school.
- Strategies for bringing technology into the classroom to increase learning.

Funds are also available to states to support the development of a state technology plan, to be integrated with the overall reform plan.

Broad-Based Involvement in Local Education Improvement Efforts

- Each local school district that applies for Goals 2000 funds will be asked to develop a broad consensus regarding a local improvement plan.
- Local districts will encourage and assist schools in developing and implementing reforms that best meet the particular needs of the schools. The local plan would include strategies for ensuring that students meet higher academic standards.

Waivers and Flexibility

- State educational agencies may apply to the U.S. Secretary of Education for waivers of certain requirements of Department of Education programs that impede the implementation of the state or local plans. States may also submit waiver requests on behalf of local school districts and schools.
- The Secretary may select up to six states for participation in an education flexibility demonstration program, which allows the Secretary to delegate his waiver authority to State education agencies.
- The Act specifies certain statutory and regulatory programmatic requirements that may not be waived, including parental involvement and civil rights laws.

Title IV. Support for Increased Parental Involvement

- This title creates parental information and resource centers to increase parents' knowledge and confidence in child-rearing activities and to strengthen partnerships between parents and professionals in meeting the educational needs of children. Parent resource centers will be funded by the U.S. Department of Education beginning in fiscal year 1995.

Title V. National Skill Standards Board

- This title creates a National Skill Standards Board to stimulate the development and adoption of a voluntary national system of occupational skill standards and certification. This Board will serve as a cornerstone of the national strategy to enhance workforce skills. The Board will be responsible for identifying broad clusters of major occupations in the U.S. and facilitating the establishment of voluntary partnerships to develop skill standards for each cluster. The Board will endorse those skill standards submitted by the partnerships that meet certain statutorily prescribed criteria.

Relationship of Goals 2000 to Other Federal Education Programs

- State participation in all aspects of the Goals 2000 Act is voluntary and is not a precondition for participation in other federal programs.

- The Goals 2000 Act is a step toward making the federal government a better partner—a supportive partner—in local and state comprehensive improvement efforts aimed at helping all children reach higher standards. The proliferation of many sets of rules and regulations for different federal education programs has often interfered with local school, community, or state efforts to improve schools. The Goals 2000 Act is designed to be flexible and supportive of community-based improvements in education.

- Other new and existing education and training programs will fit within the Goals 2000 framework of challenging academic and occupational standards, comprehensive reform, and flexibility at the state and local levels. The aim is to give schools, communities, and states the option of coordinating, promoting, and building greater coherence among federal programs and between federal programs and state and local education reforms.

- For example, the School-to-Work Opportunities Act will support state and local efforts to build a school-to-work transition system that will help youth acquire the knowledge, skills, abilities, and labor-market information they need to make a smooth transition from school to career-oriented work and to further education and training. Students in these programs could be expected to meet the same academic standards established in states under Goals 2000 and will earn portable, industry-recognized skill certificates that are benchmarked to high-quality standards.

- Similarly, the Clinton Administration's proposed reauthorization of the Elementary and Secondary Education Act (ESEA) allows states that have developed their own standards and assessments under Goals 2000 to use them for students participating in ESEA programs, thereby providing one set of standards and assessments for states and schools to use for their own reform needs and, at the same time, to meet federal requirements.

Federal Programs
for Education
and Related Activities

The following is a summary of federally funded education programs and federal laws that apply to schooling.

1787 *Northwest Ordinance* authorized land grants for the establishment of educational institutions.

1802 *An Act Fixing the Military Peace Establishment of the United States* established the U.S. Military Academy. (The U.S. Naval Academy was established in 1845 by the Secretary of the Navy.)

1862 *First Morrill Act* authorized public land grants to the states for the establishment and maintenance of agricultural and mechanical colleges.

1867 *Department of Education Act* authorized the establishment of the Department of Education.*

1876 *Appropriation Act,* Department of the Treasury established the U.S. Coast Guard Academy.

1890 *Second Morrill Act* provided for money grants for support of instruction in the agricultural and mechanical colleges.

1917 *Smith-Hughes Act* provided for grants to states for support of vocational education.

1918 *Vocational Rehabilitation Act* provided for grants for rehabilitation through training of World War I veterans.

1919 *An Act to Provide for Further Educational Facilities* authorized the sale by the federal government of surplus machine tools to educational institutions at 15 percent of acquisition cost.

1920 *Smith-Bankhead Act* authorized grants to states for vocational rehabilitation programs.

1935 *Bankhead-Jones Act* (Public Law 74–182) authorized grants to states for agricultural experiment stations.

*The Department of Education as established in 1867 was later known as the Office of Education. In 1980, under P.L. 96-88, it became a cabinet-level department. Therefore, for purposes of consistency, it is referred to as the "Department of Education" even in those tables covering years when it was officially the Office of Education. 1911 State Marine School Act authorized federal funds to be used for the benefit of any nautical school in any of eleven specified state seaport cities.
Source: National Center for Education Statistics, *Digest of Education Statistics 1996,* U.S. Department of Education, National Center for Educational Statistics.

Agricultural Adjustment Act (Public Law 74–320) authorized 30 percent of the annual customs receipts to be used to encourage the exportation and domestic consumption of agricultural commodities. Commodities purchased under this authorization began to be used in school lunch programs in 1936. The National School Lunch Act of 1946 continued and expanded this assistance.

1936   *An Act to Further the Development and Maintenance of an Adequate and Well-balanced American Merchant Marine* (Public Law 84–415) established the U.S. Merchant Marine Academy.

1937   *National Cancer Institute Act* established the Public Health Service fellowship program.

1941   *Amendment to Lanham Act of 1940* authorized federal aid for construction, maintenance, and operation of schools in federally impacted areas. Such assistance was continued under Public Law 815 and Public Law 874, 81st Congress, in 1950.

1943   *Vocational Rehabilitation Act* (Public Law 78–16) provided assistance to disabled veterans.

   School Lunch Indemnity Plan (Public Law 78–129) provided funds for local lunch food purchases.

1944   *Servicemen's Readjustment Act* (Public Law 78–346) known as the GI Bill, provided assistance for the education of veterans.

   Surplus Property Act (Public Law 78–457) authorized transfer of surplus property to educational institutions.

1946   *National School Lunch Act* (Public Law 79–396) authorized assistance through grants-in-aid and other means to states to assist in providing adequate foods and facilities for the establishment, maintenance, operation, and expansion of nonprofit school lunch programs.

   George-Barden Act (Public Law 80–402) expanded federal support of vocational education.

1948   *United States Information and Educational Exchange Act* (Public Law 80–402) provided for the interchange of persons, knowledge, and skills between the United States and other countries.

1949   *Federal Property and Administrative Services Act* (Public Law 81–152) provided for donation of surplus property to educational institutions and for other public purposes.

1950   *Financial Assistance for Local Educational Agencies Affected by Federal Activities* (Public Law 81–815 and P.L. 81–874) provided assistance for construction (Public Law 815) and operation (Public Law 874) of schools in federally affected areas.

   Housing Act (Public Law 81–475) authorized loans for construction of college housing facilities.

1954   *An Act for the Establishment of the United States Air Force Academy and Other Purposes* (Public Law 83–325) established the U.S. Air Force Academy.

   Cooperative Research Act (Public Law 83–531) authorized cooperative arrangements with universities, colleges, and state educational agencies for educational research.

   National Advisory Committee on Education Act (Public Law 83–532) established a National Advisory Committee on Education to recommend needed studies of national concern in the field of education and to propose appropriate action indicated by such studies.

   School Milk Program Act (Public Law 83–597) provided funds for purchase of milk for school lunch programs.

1956   *Library Services Act* (Public Law 84–911) provided grants to states for extension and improvement of rural public library services.

1957   *Practical Nurse Training Act* (Public Law 84–911) provided grants to states for practical nurse training.

1958   *National Defense Education Act* (Public Law 85–865) provided assistance to state and local school systems for strengthening instruction in science, mathematics, modern foreign languages, and other critical subjects; improvement of state statistical services; guidance, counseling, and testing services and training institutes; higher education student loans and fellowships; foreign language study and training provided by colleges and universities; experimentation and dissemination of information on more effective utilization of television, motion pictures, and related media for educational purposes; and vocational education for technical occupations necessary to the national defense.

Education of Mentally Retarded Children Act (Public Law 85–926) authorized federal assistance for training teachers of the handicapped.

Captioned Films for the Deaf Act (Public Law 85–905) authorized a loan service of captioned films for the deaf.

1961 *Area Redevelopment Act* (Public Law 87–27) included provisions for training or retraining of persons in redevelopment areas.

1962 *Manpower Development and Training Act* (Public Law 87–415) provided training in new and improved skills for the unemployed and underemployed.

Communications Act of 1934, Amendment (Public Law 87–447) provided grants for the construction of educational television broadcasting facilities.

Migration and Refugee Assistance Act of 1962 (Public Law 87–510) authorized loans, advances, and grants for education and training of refugees.

1963 *Health Professions Educational Assistance Act* (Public Law 88–129) provided funds to expand teaching facilities and for loans to students in the health professions.

Vocational Education Act of 1963 (Public Law 88–210) increased federal support of vocational education schools; vocational work-study programs; and research, training, and demonstrations in vocational education.

Higher Education Facilities Act of 1963 (Public Law 88–204) authorized grants and loans for classrooms, libraries, and laboratories in public community colleges and technical institutes, as well as undergraduate and graduate facilities in other institutions of higher education.

1964 *Civil Rights Act of 1964* (Public Law 88–352) authorized the Commissioner of Education to arrange for support for institutions of higher education and school districts to provide inservice programs for assisting instructional staff in dealing with problems caused by desegregation.

Economic Opportunity Act of 1964 (Public Law 88–452) authorized grants for college work-study programs for students from low-income families; established a Job Corps program and authorized support for work-training programs to provide education and vocational training and work experience opportunities in welfare programs; authorized support of education and training activities and of community action programs, including Head Start, Follow Through, and Upward Bound; and authorized the establishment of Volunteers in Service to America (VISTA) .

1965 *Elementary and Secondary Education Act* (Public Law 89–10) authorized grants for elementary and secondary school programs for children of low-income families; school library resources, textbooks, and other instructional materials for school children; supplementary educational centers and services; strengthening state education agencies; and educational research and research training.

Health Professions Educational Assistance Amendments (Public Law 89–290) authorized scholarships to aid needy students in the health professions.

Higher Education Act of 1965 (Public Law 89–329) provided grants for university community service programs, college library assistance, library training and research, strengthening developing institutions, teacher training programs, and undergraduate instructional equipment. Authorized insured student loans, established a National Teacher Corps, and provided for graduate teacher training fellowships.

Medical Library Assistance Act (Public Law 89–291) provided assistance for construction and improvement of health sciences libraries.

National Foundation on the Arts and the Humanities Act (Public Law 89–209) authorized grants and loans for projects in the creative and performing arts, and for research, training, and scholarly publications in the humanities.

National Technical Institute for the Deaf Act (Public Law 89–36) provided for the establishment, construction, equipping, and operation of a residential school for postsecondary education and technical training of the deaf.

National Vocational Student Loan Insurance Act (Public Law 89–287) encouraged state and nonprofit private institutions and organizations to establish adequate loan insurance programs to assist students to attend postsecondary business, trade, technical, and other vocational schools.

Disaster Relief Act (Public Law 89–313) provided for assistance to local education agencies to help meet exceptional costs resulting from a major disaster.

1966   *International Education Act* (Public Law 89–698) provided grants to institutions of higher education for the establishment, strengthening, and operation of centers for research and training in international studies and the international aspects of other fields of study.

National Sea Grant College and Program Act (Public Law 89–688) authorized the establishment and operation of Sea Grant Colleges and programs by initiating and supporting programs of education and research in the various fields relating to the development of marine resources.

Adult Education Act (Public Law 89–750) authorized grants to states for the encouragement and expansion of educational programs for adults, including training of teachers of adults and demonstrations in adult education (previously part of Economic Opportunity Act of 1964) .

Model Secondary School for the Deaf Act (Public Law 89–694) authorized the establishment and operation, by Gallaudet College, of a model secondary school for the deaf.

Elementary and Secondary Education Amendments of 1966 (Public Law 89–750) in addition to modifying existing programs, authorized grants to assist states in the initiation, expansion, and improvement of programs and projects for the education of handicapped children.

1967   *Education Professions Development Act* (Public Law 90–35) amended the Higher Education Act of 1965 for the purpose of improving the quality of teaching and to help meet critical shortages of adequately trained educational personnel.

Public Broadcasting Act of 1967 (Public Law 90–129) established a corporation for Public Broadcasting to assume major responsibility in channeling federal funds to noncommercial radio and television stations, program production groups, and ETV networks; conduct research, demonstration, or training in matters related to noncommercial broadcasting; and award grants for construction of educational radio and television facilities.

1968   *Elementary and Secondary Education Amendments of 1967* (Public Law 90–247) modified existing programs, authorized support of regional centers for education of handicapped children, model centers and services for deaf-blind children, recruitment of personnel and dissemination of information on education of the handicapped; technical assistance in education to rural areas; support of dropout prevention projects; and support of bilingual education programs.

Handicapped Children's Early Education Assistance Act (Public Law 90–538) authorized preschool and early education programs for handicapped children.

Vocational Education Amendments of 1968 (Public Law 90–576) modified existing programs and provided for a National Advisory Council on Vocational Education, and collection and dissemination of information for programs administered by the Commissioner of Education.

Higher Education Amendments of 1968 (Public Law 90–575) authorized new programs to assist disadvantaged college students through special counseling and summer tutorial programs, and programs to assist colleges to combine resources of cooperative programs and to expand programs that provide clinical experiences to law students.

1970   *Elementary and Secondary Education Assistance Programs, Extension* (Public Law 91–230) authorized comprehensive planning and evaluation grants to state and local education agencies; provided for the establishment of a National Commission on School Finance.

National Commission on Libraries and Information Services Act (Public Law 91–345) established a National Commission on Libraries and Information Science to effectively utilize the nation's educational resources.

Office of Education Appropriation Act (Public Law 91–380) provided emergency school assistance to desegregating local education agencies.

Environmental Education Act (Public Law 91–516) established an Office of Environmental Education to develop curriculum and initiate and maintain environmental education programs at the elementary-secondary levels; disseminate information; provide training programs for teachers and other educational, public, community, labor, and industrial leaders and employees; provide community education programs; and distribute material dealing with environment and ecology.

Drug Abuse Education Act of 1970 (Public Law 527) provided for development, demonstration, and evaluation of curriculums on the problems of drug abuse.

1971   *Comprehensive Health Manpower Training Act of 1971* (Public Law 92–257) amended Title VII of the Public Health Service Act, increasing and expanding provisions for health worker training and training facilities.

Nurse Training Act of 1971 (Public Law 92–158) amended Title VIII, Nurse Training, of the Public Health Service Act, increasing and expanding provisions for nurse training facilities.

1972   *Drug Abuse Office and Treatment Act of 1972* (Public Law 92–255) established a Special Action Office for Drug Abuse Prevention to provide overall planning and policy for all federal drug-abuse prevention functions; a National Advisory Council for Drug Abuse Prevention; community assistance grants for community mental health center for treatment and rehabilitation of persons with drug-abuse problems, and, in December 1974, a National Institute on Drug Abuse.

Education Amendments of 1972 (Public Law 92–318) established the Education Division in the U.S. Department of Health, Education, and Welfare and the National Institute of Education; general aid for institutions of higher education; federal matching grants for state student incentive grants; a national commission on financing postsecondary education; state advisory councils on community colleges; a Bureau of Occupational and Adult Education and state grants for the design, establishment, and conduct of postsecondary occupational education; and a bureau-level Office of Indian Education. Amended current Office of Education programs to increase their effectiveness and better meet special needs. Prohibited sex bias in admission to vocational, professional, and graduate schools, and public institutions of undergraduate higher education.

1973   *Older Americans Comprehensive Services Amendment of 1973* (Public Law 93–29) made available to older citizens comprehensive programs of health, education, and social services.

Comprehensive Employment and Training Act of 1973 (Public Law 93–203) provided for opportunities for employment and training to unemployed and underemployed persons. Extended and expanded provisions in the Manpower Development and Training Act of 1962, Title I of the Economic Opportunity Act of 1962, Title I of the Economic Opportunity Act of 1964, and the Emergency Employment Act of 1971 as in effect prior to June 30, 1973.

1974   *Educational Amendments of 1974* (Public Law 93–380) provided for the consolidation of certain programs; and established a National Center for Education Statistics.

Juvenile Justice and Delinquency Prevention Act of 1974 (Public Law 93–415) provided for technical assistance, staff training, centralized research, and resources to develop and implement programs to keep students in elementary and secondary schools; and established, in the Department of Justice, a National Institute for Juvenile Justice and Delinquency Prevention.

1975 *Indian Self-Determination and Education Assistance Act* (Public Law 93–638) provided for increased participation of Indians in the establishment and conduct of their education programs and services.

Harry S Truman Memorial Scholarship Act (Public Law 93–642) established the Harry S Truman Scholarship Foundation and created a perpetual education scholarship fund for young Americans to prepare and pursue careers in public service.

Indochina Migration and Refugee Assistance Act of 1975 (Public Law 94–23) authorized funds to be used for education and training of aliens who have fled from Cambodia or Vietnam.

Education of the Handicapped Act (Public Law 994–142) provided that all handicapped children have available to them a free appropriate education designed to meet their unique needs.

1976 *Educational Broadcasting Facilities and Telecommunications Demonstration Act of 1976* (Public Law 94–309) established a telecommunications demonstration program to promote the development of nonbroadcast telecommunications facilities and services for the transmission, distribution, and delivery of health, education, and public or social service information.

Education Amendments of 1976 (Public Law 94–482) extended and revised federal programs for education assistance for higher education, vocational education, and a variety of other programs.

1977 *Youth Employment and Demonstration Projects Act of 1977* (Public Law 95–93) established a youth employment training program that includes, among other activities, promoting education-to-work transition, literacy training and bilingual training, and attainment of certificates of high school equivalency.

1978 *Career Education Incentive Act* (Public Law 95–207) authorized the establishment of a career education program for elementary and secondary schools.

Tribally Controlled Community College Assistance Act (Public Law 95–471) provided federal funds for the operation and improvement of tribally controlled community colleges for Indian students.

Education Amendments of 1978 (Public Law 95–561) established a comprehensive basic skills program aimed at improving pupil achievement (replaced the existing National Reading Improvement program) ; and established a community schools program to provide for the use of public buildings.

Middle Income Student Assistance Act (Public Law 95–566) modified the provisions for student financial assistance programs to allow middle-income as well as low-income students attending college or other postsecondary institutions to qualify for federal education assistance.

1979 *Department of Education Organization Act* (Public Law 96–88) established a Department of Education containing functions from the Education Division of the Department of Health, Education, and Welfare along with other selected education programs from HEW, the Department of Justice, Department of Labor, and the National Science Foundation.

1980 *Asbestos School Hazard Protection and Control Act of 1980* (Public Law 96–270) established a program for inspection of schools for detection of hazardous asbestos materials and provided loans to assist educational agencies to contain or remove and replace such materials.

1981 *Education Consolidation and Improvement Act of 1981* (Public Law 97–35) consolidated 42 programs into 7 programs to be funded under the elementary and secondary block grant authority.

1983 *Student Loan Consolidation and Technical Amendments Act of 1983* (Public Law 98–79) established 8 percent interest rate for Guaranteed Student Loans and extended Family Contribution Schedule.

Challenge Grant Amendments of 1983 (Public Law 98–95) amended Title III, Higher Education Act, and added authorization of the Challenge Grant program. The Challenge Grant program provides funds to eligible institutions on a matching basis as incentive to seek alternative sources of funding.

Education of Handicapped Act Amendments (Public Law 98–199) added Architectural Barrier amendment and clarified participation of handicapped children in private schools.

1984 *Education for Economic Security Act* (Public Law 98–377) added new science and mathematics programs for elementary, secondary, and postsecondary education. The new programs include magnet schools, excellence in education, and equal access.

Carl D. Perkins Vocational Education Act (Public Law 98–524) continues federal assistance for vocational education through fiscal year 1989. The act replaces the Vocational Education Act of 1963. It provides aid to the states to make vocational education programs accessible to all persons, including handicapped and disadvantaged, single parents and homemakers, and the incarcerated.

Human Services Reauthorization Act (Public Law 98–558) reauthorized the Head Start and Follow Through programs through fiscal year 1986. It also created a Carl D. Perkins scholarship program, a National Talented Teachers Fellowship program, a Federal Merit Scholarships program, and a Leadership in Educational Administration program.

1985 *Montgomery GI Bill—Active Duty* (Public Law 98–525) , brought about a new GI Bill for individuals who initially entered active military duty on or after July 1, 1985.

Montgomery GI Bill—Selected Reserve (Public Law 98–525) , is an education program for members of the Selected Reserve (which includes the National Guard) who enlist, reenlist, or extend an enlistment after June 30, 1985, for a six-year period.

1986 *Handicapped Children's Protection Act* (Public Law 99–372) allows parents of handicapped children to collect attorney's fees in cases brought under the Education of the Handicapped Act and provides that the Education of the Handicapped Act does not preempt other laws, such as Section 504 of the Rehabilitation Act.

The Drug-Free Schools and Communities Act of 1986 (Public Law 99–570) , part of the Anti-Drug Abuse Act of 1986, authorizes funding for fiscal years 1987–89. Establishes programs for drug abuse education and prevention, coordinated with related community efforts and resources, through the use of federal financial assistance.

1987 *Higher Education Act Amendments of 1987* (Public Law 100–50) makes technical corrections, clarifications, or conforming amendments related to the enactment of the Higher Education Amendments of 1986.

1988 *The Augustus F. Hawkins-Robert T. Stafford Elementary and Secondary School Improvement Amendments of 1988* (Public Law 100–297) reauthorizes through 1993 major elementary and secondary education programs including: Chapter 1, Chapter 2, Bilingual Education, Math-Science Education, Magnet Schools, Impact Aid, Indian Education, Adult Education, and other smaller education programs.

Technology-Related Assistance for Individuals with Disabilities Act of 1988 (Public Law 100–407) provides financial assistance to states to develop and implement consumer-responsive statewide programs of technology-related assistance for persons of all ages with disabilities.

The Omnibus Trade and Competitiveness Act of 1988 (Public Law 100–418) authorizes new and expanded education programs. Title VI of the Act, Education and Training for American Competitiveness, authorizes new programs in literacy, math-science, foreign language, vocational training, international education, technology training, and technology transfer. The Omnibus Drug Abuse Prevention Act of 1988 (Public Law 100–690) authorizes a new teacher training program under the Drug-Free Schools and Communities Act, an early childhood education program to be administered jointly by the Departments of Health and Human Services and Education, and a pilot program for the children of alcoholics.

Stewart B. McKinney Homeless Assistance Act (Public Law 100–628) extends for two additional years programs providing assistance to the homeless, including literacy training for homeless adults and education for homeless youths.

Tax Reform Technical Amendments (Public Law 100–647) authorizes an Education Savings Bond for the purpose of postsecondary educational expenses. The bill grants tax exclusion for interest earned on regular series EE savings bonds.

1989　*The Children with Disabilities Temporary Care Reauthorization Act of 1989* (Public Law 101–127) revises and extends the programs established in the Temporary Child Care for Handicapped Children and Crises Nurseries Act of 1986.

The Drug-Free Schools and Communities Act Amendments of 1989 (Public Law 101–226) amends the Drug-Free Schools and Communities Act of 1986 to revise certain requirements relating to the provision of drug abuse education and prevention programs in elementary and secondary schools.

1990　*The Childhood Education and Development Act of 1989* (Public Law 101–239) authorized the appropriations to expand Head Start programs and programs carried out under the Elementary and Secondary Education Act of 1965 to include child-care services.

The Excellence in Mathematics, Science and Engineering Education Act of 1990 (Public Law 101–589) promotes excellence in American mathematics, science, and engineering education by creating a national mathematics and science clearinghouse, establishing regional mathematics and science education consortia, establishing three new mathematics, science, and engineering scholarship programs, and creating several other mathematics, science, and engineering education programs.

The Student Right-To-Know and Campus Security Act (Public Law 101–542) requires institutions of higher education receiving federal financial assistance to provide certain information with respect to the graduation rates of student-athletes at such institutions. The act also requires the institution to certify that it has a campus security policy and will annually submit a uniform crime report to the Federal Bureau of Investigation (FBI) .

The Children's Television Act of 1990 (Public Law 101–437) requires the Federal Communications Commission to reinstate restrictions on advertising during children's television, and enforces the obligation of broadcasters to meet the educational and informational needs of the child audience.

The Americans with Disabilities Act of 1990 (Public Law 101–336) prohibits discrimination against persons with disabilities.

The McKinney Homeless Assistance Amendments Act of 1990 (Public Law 101–645) reauthorized the Stewart B. McKinney Homeless Assistance Act programs of grants to state and local education agencies for the provision of support services to homeless children and youth.

The National Assessment of Chapter 1 Act (Public Law 101–305) requires the Secretary of Education to conduct a comprehensive national assessment of programs carried out with assistance under Chapter 1 of Title I of the Elementary and Secondary Education Act of 1965.

The Augustus F. Hawkins Human Services Reauthorization Act of 1990 (Public Law 101–510) authorized appropriations for fiscal years 1991–1994 to carry out the Head Start Act, the Follow Through Act, the Community Services Block Grant Act, and the Low-Income Home Energy Assistance Act of 1981.

The National and Community Service Act of 1989 (Public Law 101–610) increased school and college-based community service opportunities and authorized the President's Points of Light Foundation.

The School Dropout Prevention and Basic Skills Improvement Act of 1990 (Public Law 101–600) improves secondary school programs for basic skills improvements and dropout reduction.

The Medical Residents Student Loan Amendments Act of 1989 (Enacted in Public Law 101–239, the Omnibus Budget Reconciliation Act of 1989) amended the Higher Education Act of 1965 to eliminate student loan deferments for medical students serving in internships or residency programs.

The Asbestos School Hazard Abatement Reauthorization Act of 1990 (Public Law 101–637) reauthorized the Asbestos School Hazard Abatement Act of 1984, which provided financial support to elementary and secondary schools to inspect for asbestos, and to develop and implement an asbestos management plan. In addition, the act provides for programs of information, technical, and scientific assistance and training.

The Eisenhower Exchange Fellowship Program (Public Law 101–454) provided a permanent endowment for the Eisenhower Exchange Fellowship Program.

The Tribally Controlled Community College Reauthorization (Public Law 101–477) reauthorized the Tribally Controlled Community College Assistance Act and the Navajo Community College Act.

The Environmental Education Act (Public Law 101–619) promotes environmental education by the establishment of an Office of Environmental Education in the Environmental Protection Agency and the creation of several environmental education programs.

The Anti-Drug Education Act of 1990 and the Drug Abuse Resistance Education (DARE) Act of 1990 (Both bills were enacted as part of Public Law 101–647, the Comprehensive Crime Control Act of 1990.) amends the Drug-Free Schools and Communities Act and raises funding levels for schools personnel training, funds the replication of successful drug education programs, helps local education agencies to cooperate with law enforcement agencies and allows funds to be used for after-school programs. The Drug Abuse Resistance Education Act establishes a program of grants to HEW for Drug Abuse Resistance Education (DARE) programs.

The Public Service Assistance Education Act (enacted as part of Department of Defense Authorization Act, Public Law 101–510) gives federal agencies authority to provide new educational benefits to employees by paying for an employee to obtain an academic degree for which there is an agency shortage of qualified personnel, and by repaying up to $6,000 per year of the student loan of a qualified employee in exchange for a three-year commitment.

The 1990 Budget Reconciliation Act (Public Law 101–508) included a set of student aid provisions that were estimated to yield a savings of $2 billion over five years. These provisions included delayed Guaranteed Student Loan disbursements, tightened ability-to-benefit eligibility, and expanded pro rata refund policy and the elimination of student aid eligibility at high default schools.

1991   *A bill to amend title 38, United States Code, with respect to veterans education and employment programs, and for other purposes* (Public Law 102–16) revises and extends eligibility for veterans' education and employment programs.

National Literacy Act of 1991 (Public Law 102–73) established the National Institute for Literacy, the National Institute Board, and the Interagency Task Force on Literacy. Amends various federal laws to establish and extend various literacy programs.

Dire Emergency Supplemental Appropriations for Consequences of Operation Desert Shield/Desert Storm, Food Stamps, Unemployment Compensation Administration, Veterans Compensation and Pensions, and Other Urgent Needs Act of 1991 (Public Law 102–27) makes dire emergency supplemental appropriations for FY 1991 for the additional costs of Operation Desert Shield/Operation Desert Storm and other programs.

Higher Education Technical Amendments of 1991 (Public Law 102–26) amends the Higher Education Act of 1965 to resolve legal and technical issues relating to federal postsecondary student assistance programs and to prevent undue burdens on participants in Operation Desert Storm, and for other purposes.

Intelligence Authorization Act, Fiscal Year 1992 (Public Law 102–183) provides for the establishment of a National Security Education Board and a National Security Education Trust Fund within the Treasury.

National Defense Authorization Act for Fiscal Year 1992 and 1993 (Public Law 102–190) authorizes appropriations for military functions of the Department of Defense. Includes Defense Manufacturing Education program and plan for science, mathematics, and engineering education.

Rehabilitation Act Amendments of 1991 (Public Law 102–52) amends the Rehabilitation Act of 1973 to reauthorize funding for various programs, including vocational rehabilitation services, research and training, supplementary services and facilities, the National Council on Disability, the Architectural and Transportation Barriers Compliance Board, employment opportunities for individuals with handicaps, and comprehensive services for independent living. Reauthorizes funding for the Helen Keller National Center for Deaf-Blind Youths and Adults (under the Helen Keller National Center Act) and for the President's Committee on Employment of People with Disabilities.

Amend the School Dropout Demonstration Assistance Act of 1988 to extend authorization of appropriations through fiscal year 1993 and for other purposes (Public Law 102–103) revises and reauthorizes programs under: 1) the School Dropout Demonstration Assistance Act of 1988; and 2) the Star Schools Program Assistance Act. Revises the functional literacy program, and adds a life skills program, for state and local prisoners under the National Literacy Act of 1991.

A bill making appropriations for the Department of the Interior and related agencies for the fiscal year ending September 30, 1992, and for other purposes (Public Law 102–154) amends the Anti-Drug Abuse Act of 1988 to extend the authorization of appropriations for drug abuse education and prevention programs relating to youth gangs and for runaway and homeless youth. Directs the Secretary of Health and Human Services to report annually on the program of drug education and prevention relating to youth gangs.

Federal Supplemental Compensation Act of 1991 (Public Law 102–164) revises procedures for student loan debt collection.

Joint resolution to declare it to be the policy of the United States that there should be a renewed and sustained commitment by the Federal government and the American people to the importance of adult education (Public Law 102–74) declares it to be the policy of the United States that: 1) the twenty-fifth anniversary of federal aid to improve the basic and literacy skills of adults through the Adult Education Act (AEA) should be recognized and observed; and 2) there should be a continued commitment to federal aid for educating adults through AEA to increase adult literacy and assure a productive work force and a competitive United States in the twenty-first century.

National Commission on a Longer School Year Act (Public Law 102–62) establishes the National Education Commission on Time and Learning. Directs the Secretary of Education to: 1) make grants for research in the teaching of writing; and 2) carry out a program to educate students about the history and principles of the Constitution, including the Bill of Rights. Amends the Elementary and Secondary Education Act of 1965 to revise requirements for law-related education program grant and contract applications, review, and award periods. Establishes the National Council on Education Standards and Testing.

High-Performance Computing Act of 1991 (Public Law 102–194) directs the president to implement a National High-Performance Computing Program. Provides for: 1) establishment of a National Research and Education Network; 2) standards and guidelines for high-performance networks; and 3) the responsibility of certain federal departments and agencies with regard to the Network.

National and Community Service Technical Amendments Act of 1991 (Public Law 102–10) amends the National and Community Service Act to make various technical amendments.

Persian Gulf Conflict Supplemental Authorization Personnel Benefits Act of 1991 (Public Law 102–25) authorizes supplemental appropriations: 1) to the Department of Defense in connection with Operation Desert Storm; and 2) for certain national security programs. Revises various military personnel benefits provisions, especially with respect to those personnel serving on active duty in connection with Operation Desert Storm.

Veterans' Educational Assistance Amendments of 1991 (Public Law 102–127) restores certain educational benefits available to reserve and active-duty personnel under the Montgomery GI Bill to students whose course studies under such programs were interrupted by being called to active duty or given increased work in connection with the Persian Gulf War.

Individuals with Disabilities Education Act Amendments of 1991 (Public Law 102–119) amends the Individuals with Disabilities Education Act (IDEA) to extend the authorization of appropriations and revise various features of the early intervention program of services for infants and toddlers with disabilities.

National Sea Grant College Program Authorization Act of 1991 (Public Law 102–186) amends the National Sea Grant College Program Act to: 1) authorize appropriations; and 2) repeal provisions authorizing grants relating to marine affairs and resource management.

National Commission on Libraries and Information Science Act Amendments of 1991 (Public Law 102–95) amends the National Commission on Libraries and Information Science Act to revise provisions, and authorize appropriations, for the National Commission on Libraries and Information Science.

Civil Rights Act of 1991 (Public Law 102–166) amends the Civil Rights Act of 1964, the Age Discrimination in Employment Act of 1967, and the Americans with Disabilities impact, tests, mixed motives, judgment finality, foreign discrimination, seniority systems, fees, and time limits. Establishes the Technical Assistance Training Institute.

Dropout Prevention Technical Correction Amendments of 1991 (Public Law 102–159) amends federal law relating to impact aid to restore provisions for the Secretary of Education to make certain preliminary payments to local education agencies.

1992 *Higher Education Amendments of 1992* (Public Law 102–325) amends the Higher Education Act of 1965 to revise and reauthorize funding for its various programs.

Ready-To-Learn Act (Public Law 102–545) amends the General Education Provisions Act to establish Ready-To-Learn Television programs to support educational programming and support materials for preschool and elementary school children and their parents, child-care providers, and educators.

Job Training Reform Amendments of 1992 (Public Law 102–367), a bill to amend the Job Training Partnerships Act, the Carl Perkins Vocational Education Act, and the Adult Education Act.

National Commission of Time and Learning, Extension (Public Law 102–359) amends the National Education Commission on Time and Learning Act to extend the authorization of appropriations for such Commission, amends the Elementary and Secondary Education Act of 1965 to revise provisions for (1) a specified civic education program; (2) schoolwide projects for educationally disadvantaged children, and provides for additional Assistant Secretaries of Education.

1993 *Student Loan Reform Act* (Public Law 103–66) reforms the student aid process by phasing in a system of direct lending designed to provide savings for taxpayers and students. Students will be able to choose among a variety of repayment options, including income contingency.

National Service Trust Act (Public Law 103–82) amends the National and Community Service act of 1990 to establish a corporation for National Service and enhance opportunities for national service. In addition, the Act provides education grants up to $4,725 per year for 2 years to people age 17 years or older who perform community service before, during, or after postsecondary education.

Higher Education Technical Amendments Act (Public Law 103–208) amends the Higher Education Act to make technical changes and conforming amendments.

NAEP Assessment Authorization (Public Law 103–33) authorizes the use of NAEP for state-by-state comparisons.

Migrant Student Record Transfer System Extension (Public Law 103–59) extends the operation of the migrant student record transfer system.

1994 *Goals 2000: Educate America Act* (Public Law 103–227) establishes a new federal partnership through a system of grants to states and local communities to reform the nation's education system. The Act formalizes the national education goals and establishes the National Education Goals Panel. It also creates a National Education Standards and Improvement Council (NESIC) to provide voluntary national certification of state and local education standards and assessments and establishes the National Skill Standards Board to develop voluntary national skill standards.

School-To-Work Opportunities Act of 1994 (Public Law 103–239) establishes a national framework within which states and communities can develop School-To-Work Opportunities systems to prepare young people for first jobs and continuing education. The act also provides money to states and communities to develop a system of programs that include work-based learning, school-based learning, and connecting activities components. School-To-Work programs will provide students with a high school diploma (or its equivalent), a nationally recognized skill certificate, and an associate degree (if appropriate) and may lead to a first job or further education.

Safe School Act of 1994 (Part of Public Law 103–227) authorizes the award of competitive grants to local educational agencies with serious crime to implement violence prevention activities such as conflict resolution and peer mediation.

Educational Research, Development, Dissemination, and Improvement Act of 1994 (Part of Public Law 103–227) authorizes the educational research and dissemination activities of the Office of Educational Research and Improvement. The regional educational laboratories and university-based research and development centers are authorized.

Student Loan Default Exemption Extension (Public Law 103–235) amends the Higher Education Act of 1965 to extend until July 1, 1998 the effective date for cohort default rate extension for historically black colleges and universities, tribally controlled community colleges, and Navajo community colleges.

Improving America's Schools Act (Public Law 103–382) reauthorizes and revamps the Elementary and Secondary Education Act. The legislation includes Title I, the federal government's largest program providing educational assistance to disadvantaged children; professional development and technical assistance programs; a safe and drug-free schools and communities provision; and provisions promoting school equity.

1995 *Unfunded Mandate Reform Act of 1995* (Public Law 104–4) curbs the practice of imposing unfunded federal mandates on states and local governments; to strengthen the partnership between the federal government and state, local, and tribal governments, and for other purposes.

Paperwork Reduction Act of 1995 (Public Law 104–13) furthers the goals of the Paperwork Reduction Act to have federal agencies become more responsible and publicly accountable for reducing the burden of federal paperwork.

Amendment to the Elementary and Secondary Education Act of 1965 (Public Law 104–5) amends a provision of Part A of title IX of the Elementary and Secondary Education Act of 1965, relating to Indian education, to provide a technical amendment, and for other purposes.

1997 *1997 Tax Reform Law* (Public Law 105) provides $400 federal income tax deduction per child. The law establishes the Hope Scholarship that provides up to $1,500 per child tax credit for college tuition and fees per first two years of postsecondary education. A Lifetime Learning Credit was also created which enables families to claim up to 20 percent of $5,000 in tuition and fees (increasing to $10,000 in 2003). The Education IRA was established in which taxpayers may set aside up to $500 per child per year until the child reaches age 18 for funding postsecondary education.

A Bill of Rights for High School Students

Neither students nor teachers shed their constitutional rights to freedom of speech or expression at the schoolhouse gate. That has been the unmistakable holding of the Supreme Court for almost fifty years. (*Tinker* v. *Des Moines,* 1969)

The following statement of students' rights is intended as a guide to students, parents, teachers, and administrators who are interested in developing proper safeguards for student liberties. IT IS NOT A SUMMARY OF THE LAW, BUT SETS FORTH IN A GENERAL WAY WHAT THE ACLU THINKS *SHOULD* BE ADOPTED. . . .

Article I. Expression

A. Students shall be free to express themselves and disseminate their views without prior restraints through speech, essays, publications, pictures, armbands, badges, and all other media of communication. Student expression may be subject to disciplinary action only in the event that such expression creates a significant physical disruption of school activities.

B. No reporter for a student publication may be required to reveal a source of information.

C. Students shall have the right to hear speakers and presentations representing a wide range of views and subjects in classes, clubs, and assemblies. Outside speakers and presentations may be limited only by considerations of time, space, and expense.

D. Students shall be free to assemble, demonstrate, and picket peacefully, to petition and to organize on school grounds or in school buildings subject only to reasonable limitations on time, place, and manner designed to avoid significant physical obstruction of traffic or significant physical disruption of school activities.

E. Students shall be free to determine their dress and grooming as they see fit, subject only to reasonable limitations designed to protect student safety or prevent significant ongoing disruption of school activities.

F. No student shall be required to participate in any way in patriotic exercises or be penalized for refusing to participate.

Article II. Religion

A. Students shall be free to practice their own religion or no religion.

B. There shall be no school-sanctioned religious exercises or events.

C. Religious history, ideas, institutions, and literature may be studied in the same fashion as any other academic subject.

Article III. Privacy

A. Students should be free from undercover surveillance through the use of mechanical, electronic, or other secret methods, including undercover agents, without issuance of a warrant.

B. Students should be free from warrantless searches and seizures by school officials in their personal effects, lockers, or any other facilities assigned to their personal use. General housekeeping inspections of lockers and desks shall not occur without reasonable notice.

C. Student record files

1. A student's permanent record file shall include only information about academic competence and notation of the fact of participation in school clubs, sports, and other such school extracurricular activities. This file shall not be disclosed to any person or agency outside the school, except to the student's parents or guardian, without the student's permission.

2. Any other records (e.g., medical or psychological evaluations) shall be available only to the student, the student's parents or guardian, and the school staff. Such other records shall be governed by strict safeguards for confidentiality and shall not be available to others in or outside of the school even upon consent of the student.

3. A record shall be kept, and shall be available to the student, of any consultation of the student's files, noting the date and purpose of the consultation and the name of the person who consulted the files.

4. All records shall be open to challenge and correction by the student.

5. A student's opinions shall not be disclosed to any outside person or agency.

Article IV. Equality

A. No organization that officially represents the school in any capacity and no curricular or extracurricular activity organized by school authorities may deny or segregate participation or award or withhold privileges on the basis of race, color, national origin, sex, religion, creed, or opinions.

Article V. Government

A. All students may hold office and may vote in student elections. These rights shall not be denied for any reason.

B. Student government organizations and their operation, scope, and amendment procedures shall be established in a written constitution formulated with full and effective student participation.

Article VI. Due process

A. Regulations concerning student behavior shall be formulated with full and effective student participation. Such regulations shall be published and made available to all students. Regulations shall be fully, clearly, and precisely written.

B. No student shall be held accountable by school authorities for any behavior occurring outside the organized school day or off school property (except during school-sponsored events) unless such behavior presents a clear, present, and substantial ongoing danger to persons and property in the school.

C. There shall be no cruel, unusual, demeaning, or excessive punishments. There shall be no corporal punishment.

D. No student shall be compelled by school officials to undergo psychological therapy or use medication without that student's consent. No student may be required to participate in any psychological or personality testing, research project, or experiment without that student's written, informed, and willing consent. The nature, purposes, and possible adverse consequences of the testing, project, or experiment shall be fully explained to the student.

E. A student shall have the right to due process in disciplinary and investigative proceedings. In cases that may involve serious penalties, such as suspension for more than three days, expulsion, transfer to another school, a notation on the student's record, or long-term loss of privileges:

1. A student shall be guaranteed a formal hearing before an impartial board. That student shall have the right to appeal hearing results.
2. Rules for hearings and appeals shall be written and published, and there shall be full and effective student participation in their formulation.
3. The student shall be advised in writing of any charges brought against that student.
4. The student shall have the right to present evidence and witnesses and to cross-examine adverse witnesses. The student shall have the right to have an advisor of his or her own choosing present.
5. The hearing shall be open or private as the student chooses.
6. The student shall have a reasonable time to prepare a defense.
7. A student may not be compelled to incriminate himself or herself.
8. The burden of proof, beyond a reasonable doubt, shall be upon the school.
9. A written record of all hearings and appeals shall be made available to the student, at the school's expense.
10. A student shall be free from double jeopardy.

Domains
of Learning

The levels of cognitive learning evaluate depth of learning. The levels are numbered from the most superficial to the most advanced.

1.00 Knowledge
    1.10 Knowledge of specifics
    1.20 Knowledge of ways and means of dealing with specifics
    1.30 Knowledge of the universals and abstractions in a field

2.00 Comprehension
    2.10 Translation
    2.20 Interpretation
    2.30 Extrapolation

3.00 Application

4.00 Analysis

4.10 Analysis of elements
4.20 Analysis of relationships
4.30 Analysis of organizational principles

5.00 Synthesis
    5.10 Production of a unique communication
    5.20 Production of a plan or proposed set of operations
    5.30 Derivation of a set of abstract relations

6.00 Evaluation
    6.10 Judgments in terms of internal evidence
    6.20 Judgments in terms of external criteria

Source: Benjamin S. Bloom, ed., *Taxonomy of Educational Objectives* (New York: Longmans, Green, 1956), pp. 6–8.

Different levels of affective learning are classified as follows:

1.00 Receiving (attending)
    1.10 Awareness
    1.20 Willingness to receive
    1.30 Controlled or selected attention

2.00 Responding
    2.10 Acquiescence in responding
    2.20 Willingness to respond
    2.30 Satisfaction in response

3.00 Valuing
    3.10 Acceptance of a value

3.20 Preference for a value
3.30 Commitment

4.00 Organization
    4.10 Conceptualization of a value
    4.20 Organization of a value system

5.00 Characterization by a value or value complex
    5.10 Generalized set
    5.20 Characterization

Source: David R. Krathwohl, Benjamin S. Bloom, and Bertram B. Masia, eds. *Taxonomy of Educational Objectives* (New York: McKay, 1964), pp. 176–193.

Levels of learning for the psychomotor domain are as follows:

1.00 Reflex movements
    1.10 Segmental reflexes
    1.20 Intersegmental reflexes
    1.30 Suprasegmental reflexes

2.00 Basic-fundamental movements
    2.10 Locomotor movements
    2.20 Nonlocomotor movements
    2.30 Manipulative movements

3.00 Perceptual abilities
    3.10 Kinesthetic discrimination
    3.20 Visual discrimination
    3.30 Auditory discrimination
    3.40 Tactile discrimination
    3.50 Coordinated abilities

4.00 Physical abilities
    4.10 Endurance
    4.20 Strength
    4.30 Flexibility
    4.40 Agility

5.00 Skilled movements
    5.10 Simple adaptive skills
    5.20 Compound adaptive skills
    5.30 Complex adaptive skills

6.00 Nondiscursive communication
    6.10 Expressive movement
    6.20 Interpretive movement

Source: Anita J. Harrow, *A Taxonomy of the Psychomotor Domain* (New York: McKay, 1972), pp. 1–2.

Professional Journals

American Educational Research Journal
American Educational Research Association, 1230 17th Street NW, Washington, D.C. 20036
(202) 223-9485

American Educator
American Federation of Teachers, Local 231 AFL-CIO 7451 Thira, Detroit, MI 48202
(202) 797-4400

American Middle School Education
National Middle School Institute, Box 16149, Columbus, OH 43216
(614) 369-8005

American School Board Journal
National School Boards Association, 1680 Duke Street, Alexandria, VA 22314
(703) 838-6722

Arts and Activities
Publishers Development Corporation, 591 Camino de la Reina, Suite 200, San Diego, CA 92108
(619) 297-8520

Behavioral Disorders Journal
Council for Exceptional Children, 1920 Association Drive, Reston, VA 22091
(703) 620-3660

Business Education World
McGraw-Hill, Inc., 1221 Avenue of the Americas, New York, NY 10020
(212) 512-4736

Cable in the Classroom
I D G Peterborough, 80 Elm Street, Peterborough, NH 03458
(603) 924-0100

Canadian Council of Teachers of English Newletter
Canadian Council of Teachers of English, Box 4520 Sta. C, Calgary Alta. T2T 5N3, Canada
(403) 244-4487

Canadian Journal of Education
Canadian Society for The Study of Education, 14 Henderson Avenue, Ottawa Ont. K1N 7P1, Canada
(613) 230-3532

Canadian Social Studies
Faculty of Education, 4-116 Education N., Edmonton, Alta. T6G 2G5, Canada
FAX (403) 492-0236

Canadian Vocational Journal
Canadian Vocational Association, PO Box 3435, Station D, Ottawa Ont. K1P 6L4, Canada
(613) 596-2515

Catalyst for Change
(National School Development Council) East Texas School Study

Council, East Texas State University, Commerce, TX 75428
(903) 886-5521

Challenge
Good Apple, 1204 Buchanan Street, Box 299, Carthage, IL 62321-0299
(217) 357-3981

Childhood Education
Association for Childhood Education International, 11141 Georgia Avenue, Suite 200, Wheaton, MD 20902
(301) 942-2443

Clearing House
Heldref Publications, 4000 Albemarle Street NW, Washington, D.C. 20016
(202) 362-6445

Cognition and Instruction
Lawrence Erlbaum Associates, 365 Broadway, Hillsdale, NJ 07642
(201) 666-4110

Computers & Education
Pergamon Press, Inc., Journals Division, 660 White Plains Road, Tarrytown, NY 10591-5153
(914) 524-9200

Computers in Education Journal
American Society for Engineering Education, Computers in Education Division, Box 68, Port Royal Square, Port Royal, VA 22535
(804) 742-5611

Computers in the Schools
Haworth Press, Inc., 10 Alice Street, Binghamton, NY 13904
(800) 342-9678

The Computing Teacher
International Council for Computers in Education, University of Oregon, 1787 Agate Street, Eugene, OR 97403
(503) 686-4414

Creative Classroom
Children's Television Workshop, One Lincoln Plaza, New York, NY 10023
(212) 595-3456

Curriculum Review
Curriculum Review Company, 212 West Superior Street, Suite 200, Chicago, IL 60610-3533
(312) 922-8245

Dialogue in Instrumental Music Education
D I M E, Humanities Building, School of Music, University of Wisconsin, Madison, WI 53706-1483
(608) 263-3220

Early Years
Trentham Books Ltd, Westview House, 734 London Road, Oakhill, Stoke-on-Trent, Staffs. ST4 5NP, England
0782-745567/FAX 0782-745553

Education Digest
Prakken Publications, PO Box 8623, Ann Arbor, MI 48107
(313) 769-1211

Educational Leadership
Association for Supervision and Curriculum Development, 225 North Washington Street, Alexandria, VA 22314
(703) 549-9110

Educational Measurement, Issues and Practice
National Council on Measurement in Education, 1230 17th Street NW, Washington, D.C. 20036
(202) 223-9318

Educational Technology
Educational Technology Publications, 720 Palisade Avenue, Englewood Cliffs, NJ 07632
(201) 871-4007

Electronic Learning
Scholastic Inc., 730 Broadway, New York, NY 10003-9538
(212) 505-3000

The Elementary School Journal
University of Chicago Press, PO Box 37005, Chicago, IL 60637
(312) 962-7600

English in Education
National Association for the Teaching of English, Birley School Annexe, Fox Lane Site, Frecheville, Sheffield S12 4WY, England
0742-390081

English Journal
National Council of Teachers in English, 1111 Kenyon Road, Urbana, IL 61801

Exceptional Children
Council for Exceptional Children, 1920 Association Drive, Reston, VA 22091
(703) 620-3660

Exceptionality Education Canada
University of Calgary Press, 2500 University Drive NW, Calgary, Alta. T2N 1N4, Canada
(403) 220-7578

Feminist Teacher
Feminist Teacher, Ballantine 442 Indiana University, Bloomington, IN 47405
(812) 855-3042

Focus on Exceptional Children
Love Publishing Company, 1777 South Bellaire Street, Denver, CO 80222
(303) 757-2579

Guide to Federal Funding for Education
Education Funding Research Council, 4301 Fairfax Drive Number 875, Arlington, VA 22203-1627
(703) 528-1000

Harvard Educational Review
Harvard Educational Review, 6 Appian Way, Suite 349, Gutman Library, Cambridge, MA 02138
(617) 495-3432

The High School Journal
University of North Carolina Press, Box 2288, Chapel Hill, NC 27515-2288
(919) 966-3561

History of Education Quarterly
School of Education, Indiana University, Bloomington, IN 47405
(812) 855-9334

Human Communication and Its Disorders
Ablex Publishing Corporation, 355 Chestnut Street, Norwood, NJ 07648
(201) 767-8450

Instructor
Instructor, 545 Fifth Avenue, New York, NY 10017
(212) 503-2888

The International Schools Journal
European Council of International Schools, 21B Lavant Street, St Petersfield Hampshire GU32 3EL, England

Journal of American Indian Education
Arizona State University, College of Education, Bureau of Educational Research and Services, Tempe, AZ 85281
(602) 965-6292

Journal of Childhood Communication Disorders
Council for Exceptional Children, Division for Children with Communication Disorders, 1920 Association Drive, Reston, VA 22091-1589
(703) 620-3660

Journal of Curriculum and Supervision
Association for Supervision and Curriculum Development, 225 North Washington Street, Alexandria, VA 22314
(703) 549-9110

Journal of Early Intervention
Special Press, 474 North Lake Shore Drive, Number 3910, Chicago, IL 60611-3400
(312) 446-0500

Journal of Education
Boston University, School of Education, 605 Commonwealth Avenue, Boston, MA 02215
(617) 353-3230

Journal of Educational Measurement
National Council on Measurement in Education, 1230 17th Street NW, Washington, D.C. 20036
(202) 223-9318

Journal of Educational Psychology
American Psychological Association, 1400 North Uhle Street, Arlington, VA 22201
(703) 247-7703

Journal of Educational Research
Heldref Publications, 4000 Albemarle Street NW, Washington, DC 20016
(202) 362-6445

Journal of Learning Disabilities
Pro-Ed Inc, 8700 Shoal Creek Boulevard, Austin, TX 78757-6897
(512) 451-3246

Journal of Moral Education
Carfax Publishing Company, PO Box 25 Abingdon, Oxfordshire OX14 3UE, England
US subscriptions: 85 Ash Street, Hopkinton, MA 01748
(508)-580-6784

Journal of Multicultural Counseling and Development
American Association for Counseling Development, 5999 Stevenson Avenue, Alexandria, VA 22304

Journal of Physical Education, Recreation and Dance
American Alliance for Health, Physical Education, Recreation, and Dance, 1990 Association Drive, Reston, VA 22091
(703) 476-3400

Journal of Reading
International Reading Association, 800 Barksdale Road, Newark, DE 19714-8139
(800) 336-READ

Journal of Rural and Small Schools
West Washington University, Miller Hall 359, Bellingham, WA 98225
(206) 676-3576

Journal of School Psychology
Pergamon Press Inc, Maxwell House, Fairview Park, Elmsford, NY 10523.
Canada subscriptions: 150 Consumers Road, Suite 104, Willowdale Ontario M2J 1P9, Canada
(914) 592-7700

Journal for Vocational Special Needs Education
National Association of Vocational Education Special Needs Personnel, 518 East Nebraska Hall, University of Nebraska, Lincoln, NE 68508-0515
(402) 472-2365

Journal of Vocational and Technical Education
Omicron Tau Theta, 215 Lane Hall, Blacksburg, VA 24061
(703) 231-5471

Language Arts
National Council of Teachers of English, 1111 Kenyon Road, Urbana, IL 61801
(217) 328-3870

Learning
Education Today Company, Inc., 530 University Avenue, Palo Alto, CA 94301
(650) 646-8700

Lectura y Vida
International Reading Association, Inc., 800 Barksdale Road, Box 8139, Newark, DE 19714-8139
(302) 731-1600

Mathematics in School
Longman Group UK Ltd., Westgate House, The High, Harlow, Essex CM20 1YR, England
0279-442601

Mathematics Teacher
National Council of Teachers of Mathematics, 1906 Association Drive, Reston, VA 22091
(703) 620-9840

Mathematics Teaching
Association of Teachers of Mathematics, 7 Shaftesbury Street, Derby DE3 8YB, England
0332-46599

Media and Methods
American Society of Educators, 1429 Walnut Street, Philadelphia, PA 19102
(215) 563-3501

Microcomputers in Education
John Mongillo, Editor & Publisher, 1125 Point Judith Road, Apartment E7, Narragansett, RI 02882-5541
(203) 655-3798

Middle School Journal
National Middle School
Association, 4807 Evanswood
Drive, Columbus, OH 43229-6292
(614) 848-8211

Minority Funding Report
Government Information Services,
4301 Fairfax Drive Suite 875,
Arlington, VA 22203-1627
(703) 528-1000

NASSP Bulletin
National Association of Secondary
School Principals, 1904 Association
Drive, Reston, VA 22091-1598
(703) 860-0200

NEA Today
National Education Association,
1201 16th Street NW, Washington,
D.C. 20036

Perspectives in Education and Deafness
Gallaudet University, Pre-College
Programs, KDES PAS-6, 800 Florida
Avenue NE, Washington, D.C.
20002-3695
(202) 651-5340

Philosophy of Education
Philosophy of Education Society,
Illinois State University, Normal, IL
61761
(309) 438-5422

Principal
National Association of Elementary
School Principals, 1615 Duke Street,
Alexandria, VA 22314
(703) 684-3345

PTA Communicator
Texas Congress of Parents and
Teachers, 408 West 11th Street,
Austin, TX 78701
(512) 476-6769

PTA Today
National Congress of Parents and
Teachers, 700 North Rush Street,
Chicago, IL 60611
(312) 787-0977

Reading Horizons
College of Education, Western
Michigan University, Kalamazoo,
MI 49008
(616) 387-3470

Reading Improvement
Project Innovation, 1362 Santa Cruz
Court, Chula Vista, CA 92010

Reading Psychology
Taylor & Francis, 1900 Frost Road,
Suite 101, Bristol, PA 19007-1598
(800) 821-8312

Reading Research and Instruction
College Reading Association,
Department of Curriculum &
Instruction, Pittsburg State
University, Pittsburg, KS 66762
(316) 235-4494

Reading Research Quarterly
International Reading Association,
Inc., 800 Barksdale Road, Box 8139,
Newark, DE 19714-8139
(302) 731-1600

Reading Teacher
International Reading Association,
Inc., 800 Barksdale Road, Box 8139,
Newark, DE 19714-8139
(302) 731-1600

Rural Special Education Quarterly
National Rural Project, Western
Washington University,
Bellingham, WA 98225
(206) 676-3576

School Arts
Davis Publications Inc, 50 Portland
Street, Printers Building, Worcester,
MA 01608
(508) 754-7201

The School Counselor
American Association for
Counseling Development, 5999
Stevenson Avenue, Alexandria, VA
22304
(703) 823-9800

*School Library Media Folders of Ideas
for Library Excellence*
Libraries Unlimited, Inc., Box 3988,
Englewood, CO 80155-3988

Science and Children
National Science Teachers
Association, 1742 Connecticut
Avenue NW, Washington, D.C.
20009
(202) 328-5800

Social Studies and the Young Learner
National Council for the Social
Studies, 3501 Newark Street, NW,
Washington, D.C. 20016
(202) 966-7840

Teaching Exceptional Children
Council for Exceptional Children,
1920 Association Drive, Reston, VA
22091
(703) 620-3660

Teaching Pre K–8
Early Years, Inc., 325 Post Road
West, Westport, CT 06880

Urban Education
SAGE Publications Inc, 2111 West
Hillcrest Drive, Newbury Park, CA
91320
(805) 499-0721

Free Resources

Apple Education News
Apple Computer, Inc.,
10381 Bandley Drive,
Cupertino, CA 95014
(408) 974-2552

G P N Educational Video Catalog,
Elementary-Secondary
Great Plains National Instructional
Television Library, Box 80669,
Lincoln, NE 68501
(402) 472-2007

Journal of Outdoor Education
Journal of Outdoor Education c/o
The Editor, Box 299, Oregon, IL
61061
(815) 732-2111

Educators Grade Guide to Free
Teaching Aids ($44.95)
Educators Guide to Free Films,
Filmstrips, and Slides ($32.95)
Educators Guide to Free Guidance
Materials ($28.95)
Educators Guide to Free Health,
Physical Education & Recreation
Materials ($27.95)

Educators Guide to Free Science
Materials ($27.95)
Educators Guide to Free Social
Studies Materials ($28.95)
Educators Guide to Free Videotapes
($27.95)
Educators Index of Free Materials
($46.95)
All from
Educators Progress Service Inc,
214 Center Street, Randolph, WI
53956
(414) 326-3126 (plus $3.95 per guide
for postage and handling)

Professional Organizations

American Alliance for Health, Physical Education, Recreation and Dance (AAHPERD)
1900 Association Dr., Reston, VA 22091
(703) 476-3400
http://www.aahperd.org

American Association of Physics Teachers (AAPT)
5112 Berwyn Rd., College Park, MD 20740
(301) 345-4200
http://www.aapt.org

American Association of School Administrators (AASA)
1801 N. Moore St., Arlington, VA 22209
(703) 528-0700
http://www.aasa.org

American Association of Teachers of French (AATF)
57 E. Armory Ave., Champaign, IL 61820
(217) 333-2842
http://www.aatf.org

American Association of Teachers of Spanish and Portuguese (AATSP)
PO Box 6349, Mississippi State, MS 39762
(601) 325-2041
http://www.aatsp.org

American Montessori Society (AMS)
150 5th Ave., Ste. 203, New York, NY 10011
(212) 924-3209

American Schools Association (ASA)
3069 Amwiler Rd., Ste. 4, Atlanta, GA 30360
(404) 449-7141
http://www.asa.org

American String Teachers Association (ASTA)
4020 McEwen, No. 105, Dallas, TX 75244
(214) 233-3116
http://www.asta.org

American Vocational Association (AVA)
1410 King St., Alexandria, VA 22314
(703) 683-3111
http://www.ava.org

Association for Childhood Education International (ACEI)
11501 Georgia Ave., Ste. 312 Wheaton, MD 20902
(301) 942-2443

Association for Supervision and Curriculum Development (ASCD)
1250 N. Pitt St., Alexandria, VA 22314-1403
(703) 549-9110
http://www.ascd.org/

Association for World Travel Exchange (AWTE)
38 W. 88th St., New York, NY 10024
(212) 787-7706

Business Professionals of America
5454 Cleveland Ave., Columbus, OH 43231
(614) 895-7277

College Reading and Learning Association (CRLA)
Chemekata Community College, PO Box 14007 Salem, OR 97309
(503) 399-2556
http://www.crla.org

Council for Children with Behavioral Disorders (CCBD)
c/o Council for Exceptional Children 1920 Association Dr., Reston, VA 22091-1589
(703) 620-3660
http://www.ccbd.org

Council for Exceptional Children (CEC)
1920 Association Dr., Reston, VA 22091-1589
(703) 620-3660
http://www.cec.sped.org

Cousteau Society, The (TCS)
870 Greenbriar Cir., Ste. 402, Chesapeake, VA 23320
(804) 523-9335

Distributive Education Clubs of
America (DECA)
1908 Association Dr., Reston, VA
22091
(703) 860-5000

Division on Mental Retardation of
the Council for Exceptional
Children (CEC-MR)
245 Cedar Springs Dr., Athens, GA
30605
(706) 546-6132
http://www.cec.sped.org

Earthwatch
680 Mt. Auburn St., Box 403,
Watertown, MA 02272
(617) 926-8200

Educational Theatre Association
(ETA)
3368 Central Pky., Cincinnati, OH
45225-2392
(513) 559-1996

Federation Internationale des
Mouvements d'Ecole Moderne
(FIMEM)
Wilhelm-Leuschnerstrasse 6B,
W-4350 Recklinghausen, Germany
2361-42501

Future Homemakers of America
1910 Association Dr., Reston, VA
22091
(703) 476-4900

German Teachers Association
(GTA)
Nordstrasse 53, W-5300 Bonn 1,
Germany
(228) 231266

International Reading Association
(IRA)
800 Barksdale Rd., PO Box 8139
Newark, DE 19714-8139
(302) 731-1600
http://www.ira.org

International Thespian Society (ITS)
3368 Central Pky., Cincinnati, OH
45225-2392
(513) 559-1996

Investment Education Institute (IEI)
1515 E. 11 Mile Rd., Royal Oak, MI
48067
(313) 543-0612

Junior Achievement
1 Education Way
Colorado Springs, CO 80906
(719) 540-8000
http://www.ja.org

Music Teachers National
Association (MTNA)
617 Vine St., Ste. 1432
Cincinnati, OH 45202
(513) 421-1420

National Art Education Association
(NAEA)
1916 Association Dr.,
Reston, VA 22091-1590
(703) 860-8000

National Association for the
Education of Young Children
(NAEYC)
1834 Connecticut Ave. NW
Washington, D.C. 20009
(202) 232-8777
http://www.naeyc.org/

National Association for Girls and
Women in Sport (NAGWS)
1900 Association Dr.,
Reston, VA 22091
(703) 476-3450

National Association for Sport and
Physical Education (NASPE)
1900 Association Dr.,
Reston, VA 22091
(703) 476-3410

National Association of Elementary
School Principals (NAESP)
1615 Duke St.,
Alexandria, VA 22314
(703) 684-3345
http://www.naesp.org

National Association of Partners in
Education (NAPE)
209 Madison St., Ste. 401
Alexandria, VA 22314
(703) 836-4880

National Association of Secondary
School Principals
(NASSP)
1904 Association Dr.,
Reston, VA 22091
(703) 860-0200
http://www.nassp.org

National Association of Student
Activity Advisers (NASAA)
1904 Association Dr., Reston, VA
22090
(703) 860-0200

National Business Education
Association (NBEA)
1914 Association Dr.,
Reston, VA 22091
(703) 860-8300
http://www.nbea.org

National Catholic Educational
Association (NCEA)
1077 30th St. NW, Ste. 100
Washington, D.C. 20007
(202) 337-6232
http://www.ncea.org

National Council for the Social
Studies (NCSS)
3501 Newark St. NW
Washington, D.C. 20016
(202) 966-7840
http://www.ncss.org

National Council of Teachers of
English (NCTE)
1111 Kenyon Rd., Urbana, IL 61801
(217) 328-3870
http://www.ncte.org

National Council of Teachers of
Mathematics (NCTM)
1906 Association Dr.,
Reston, VA 22091-1593
(703) 620-9840
http://www.nctm.org

National FFA Organization
(NFFAO)
National FFA Center, Box 15160,
5632 Mt. Vernon Memorial Hwy.
Alexandria, VA 22309-0160
(703) 360-3600
http://www.agriculture.com/
contents/FFA/index.html

National Forensic League (NFL)
PO Box 38, Ripon, WI 54971
(414) 748-6206

National Head Start Association
(NHSA)
201 N. Union St., Ste. 320
Alexandria VA 22314
(703) 739-0875
http://www.nhsa.org

National Middle School
Association (NMSA)
4807 Evanswood Dr.,
Columbus, OH 43229
(614) 848-8211
http://www.nmsa.org

National PTA — National Congress
of Parents and Teachers
700 N. Rush St., Chicago, IL 60611
(312) 787-0977
http://www.pta.org

National Science Teachers
Association (NSTA)
1742 Connecticut Ave. NW
Washington, D.C. 20009-1171
(202) 328-5800
http://www.nsta.org

National Student Nurses'
Association (NSNA)
555 W. 57th St., Ste. 1327
New York, NY 10019
(212) 581-2211
http://www.nsna.org/

National Vocational Agricultural
Teachers' Association (NVATA)
PO Box 15440,
Alexandria, VA 22309
(703) 780-1862

Plymouth Rock Foundation (PRF)
Fisk Mill, PO Box 577
Marlborough, NH 03455
(603) 876-4685

Quest International
537 Jones Rd., PO Box 566
Granville, OH 43023-0566
(614) 552-6400

Teachers of English to Speakers of
Other Languages (TESOL)
1600 Cameron St., Ste. 300
Alexandria, VA 22314-2751
(703) 836-0774
http://www.tesol.edu/.

Technology Student Association
(TSA)
1914 Association Dr.,
Reston, VA 22091
(703) 860-9000

Vocational Industrial Clubs of
America (VICA)
PO Box 3000, Leesburg, VA 22075
(703) 777-8810

Current Minimum Requirements for Earning an Initial Certificate for Teaching Public Elementary and Secondary Schools

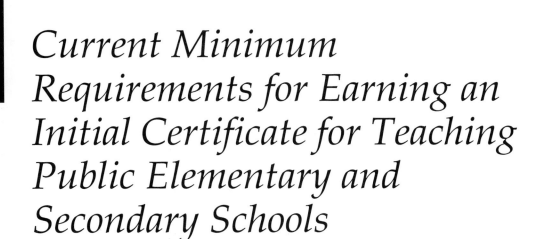

State	College B.A. Degree	General Ed. as Specified by SEA	Pedagogical Studies as Specified by SEA	Studies of Subject Matter as Specified by SEA	Pedagogical Studies as Specified by SEA	Basic Skills in Reading	Basic Skills in Mathematics	Basic Skills in Writing	Examination of Teaching Proficiency	Examination of Subject Matter Knowledge	Other
	1	2	3	4	5	6	7	8	9	10	11
Alabama	x	x	x	x	x	x	x	x		x	(1)
Alaska	x										
Arizona	x	x	x	x	x	x	x^1	x^1	x		
Arkansas	x	x	x	x	x					x	(1)
California	x			x	x	x	x	x		x^1	
Colorado	x	x	x	x	x			x	(2)		(1)
Connecticut	x	x			x	x^1	x^1				
Delaware	x					x	x	x			(1)
Dist. of Columbia	x	x	x	x	x						
Florida	x	x		x	x	x	x	x	x		
Georgia	x	x	x	x	x	x^1	x^1			x^2	
Hawaii	x					x	x	x			
Idaho	x	x	x	x	x	x^1					
Illinois	x	x	x	x	x						
Indiana	x	x	x	x	x						
Iowa	x	x	x	x	x						
Kansas	x	x	x	x	x				x^1		
Kentucky	x	x		x	x	x	x	x	x^1	x^1	

	College B.A. Degree	General Ed. as Specified by SEA	Pedagogical Studies as Specified by SEA	Studies of Subject Matter as Specified by SEA	Pedagogical Studies as Specified by SEA	Basic Skills in Reading	Basic Skills in Mathematics	Basic Skills in Writing	Examination of Teaching Proficiency	Examination of Subject Matter Knowledge	Other
Louisiana	x	x		x						x	
Maine	x	x		x^1	x	x^2					
Maryland	x	x^1		x	x						
Massachusetts	x			x	x						
Michigan	x	x	x	x	x						
Minnesota	x	x	x	x^1	x	x^2	x^2	x^2			
Mississippi	x	x	x^1	x	x	x	x	x	x	x	(2)
Missouri	x	x	x	x	x						
Montana	x	x	x	x	x	x	x^1	x			
Nebraska	x	x	x	x	x	x	x	x		x	
Nevada	x	x	x	x	x	x	x^1	x		x^2	
New Hampshire	x	x	x	x	x	x	x	x			
New Jersey	x	x	x	x	x	x	x	x	x	x^1	
New Mexico	x					x	x	x			
New York	x			x^1	x	x^2					
N. Carolina	x	x	x	x	x	x	x	x	x	x	
N. Dakota	x	x	x	x	x						(1)
Ohio	x	x		x	x	x	x	x		x^1	(2)
Oklahoma	x	x	x	x	x	x^1	x^1	x^1		x	
Oregon	x			x	x	x	x^1	x			
Pennsylvania	x										(1)
Rhode Island	x			x^1							
S. Carolina	x	x	x	x	x	x	x	x		x	
S. Dakota	x	x	x	x	x						
Tennessee	x	x	x	x	x	x	x	x			(1)
Texas	x	x		x	x	x^1	x^1	x^1	·	(2)	
Utah	x	x		x	x						(1)
Vermont	x	x	x	x	x	x	x	x			
Virginia	x	x	x	x	x	x	x	x	x	x	
Washington	x	x	x	x	x	x	x	x	x^1	x^1	
W. Virginia	x	x		x	x	x	x^1				
Wisconsin	x	x	x	x	x						
Wyoming	x	x	x	x	x						

From *In the Classroom: An Introduction to Education* by J. S. Reed and V. E. Bergemann, 1992, pp. 544–547. © 1992 by The Dushkin Publishing Group, Inc. All rights reserved. Reprinted by permission.

Footnotes

Alabama
1. Exam of knowledge of concepts common to all teaching areas (including mainstreaming).

Arizona
1. Elementary level only.

Arkansas
1. NTE Professional Knowledge for both Elementary and Secondary.

California
1. Exempted from exam if completed a Commission-approved subject matter program.

Colorado
1. Six semester hours of recent course work (within the past five years).
2. Basic skills in oral English and written English but no writing sample required.

Connecticut
1. Elementary level only.

Delaware
1. Vocational Ed Skills Test for Secondary Vocational Ed Program.

Georgia
1. Elementary level only.
2. On-the-job assignment for both levels.

Idaho
1. Elementary level only.

Kansas
1. Examination required beginning May 1986.

Kentucky
1. Effective 1985–86 school year and thereafter.

Maine
1. Secondary level only.
2. Elementary level only.

Minnesota
1. Secondary level only.
2. Elementary level only.

Mississippi
1. Elementary level only.
2. National Teachers' Exam.

Montana
1. Elementary level only.

Nevada
1. Elementary level only.
2. Exams are given at the I.H.E (Institute of Higher Education).

New Jersey

1. As of September 1, 1985.

New York

1. Secondary level only.
2. Elementary level only.

North Dakota

1. North Dakota Native American Studies.

Ohio

1. Secondary level only.
2. Applicants for both Elementary and Secondary Certificates must complete an approved program.

Oklahoma

1. Student must show proficiency in reading, writing, and mathematics prior to admission to an approved program. The college assesses for those skills.

Oregon

1. Elementary level only.

Pennsylvania

1. Completion of an approved program and a recommendation by a college are required. Currently Pennsylvania's teacher certification standards are being revised. More specific requirements may be established in the future.

Rhode Island

1. Secondary level only.

Tennessee

1. All three sections of the NTE Commons Exam.

Texas

1. As of May 1, 1984, Pass/Fail level on these tests is required for admission to the institution's program.
2. Certification examinations are required at all levels as of May 1, 1986.

Utah

1. Metric competencies and reading/reading in content fields.

Washington

1. These exams are not formal, uniform state examinations. Rather, an assessment in the programs.

West Virginia

1. Elementary level only.

Education Agencies and Certification Offices (by state)

Note: Be sure to address correspondence to the State Teacher Certification office.

Alabama
Department of Education
Gordon Persons Office Building
50 North Ripley Street
Montgomery, AL 36130-3901
(205) 242-9977
http://www.alsde.edu

Alaska
Department of Education
P.O. Box F
801 West 10th Street, Suite 200
Juneau, AK 99801-1894
(907) 465-2810
http://www.educ.state.ak.us

American Samoa
Department of Education
Pago Pago, AS 96799
(OS) 684-633-5237
none

Arizona
Department of Public Instruction
P.O. Box 25609
1535 West Jefferson
Phoenix, AZ 85007
(602) 542-4368
http://ade.state.az.us

Arkansas
Department of Education
4 State Capitol Mall
Little Rock, AR 72201-1071
(501) 682-4342
http://arkedu.ik12.ar.us/

California
Department of Education
721 Capitol Mall
Sacramento, CA 95814
(916) 657-5485
http://goldmine.cde.ca.gov

Commission on Teaching
Credentialing
Box 944270
Sacramento, CA 94244-7000
(916) 445-7254
http://goldmine.cde.ca.gov

Colorado
Department of Education
210 E. Colfax Avenue
Denver, CO 80203
(303) 866-6628
http://www.
cde.state.co.us

Connecticut
Department of Education
Box 2219
Hartford, CT 06145-2219
(860) 566-5201
http://www.aces.k12.ct.us/csdf

Delaware
Department of Public Instruction
P.O. Box 1402, Townsend Bldg. No.
279
Federal and Lockeman Streets
Dover, DE 19903
(302) 739-4688
http://www.dpi.state.de.us

Department of Defense Dependents Schools
Department of Defense
Office of Dependents Schools
1225 Jefferson Davis Hall
Crystal Gateway #2, Suite 1500
Alexandria, VA 22202
(703) 746-7844
http://www.ed.gov/pubs/
AchGoal/1/dod.html

District of Columbia
Division of State Services Teacher
Education
415 12th Street, N.W., Room 1013
Washington, D.C. 20004
(202) 724-4246
http://www.K12.dc.us

Florida
Department of Education
Room PL 08, Capitol Bldg.
Tallahassee, FL 32301
(904) 487-1785
http://www.firn.edu/doe/
index.html

Bureau of Teacher Certification
Florida Education Center
325 W. Gaines, Room 201
Tallahassee, FL 32399
(904) 488-2317
http://www.firn.edu/doe/
index.html

Georgia
Department of Education
2066 Twin Towers East
Atlanta, GA 30334-5020
(404) 657-9000
http://www.doe.k12.ga.us

Guam
Department of Education
P.O. Box DE
Agana, GM 96910
(OS) 671-472-8901
none

Hawaii
Department of Education
P.O. Box 2360
Honolulu, HI 96804
(808) 586-3420
http://www.K12.hi.us

Idaho
Department of Education
L.B. Jordan Office Bldg.
650 West State Street
Boise, ID 83720-3650
(208) 334-3475
http://www.sde.state.id.us

Illinois
Board of Education
100 North First Street
Springfield, IL 62777
(217) 782-4321
http://www.isbe.state.il.us

Indiana
Teacher Licensing
251 East Ohio Street, Suite 201
Indianapolis, IN 46204-2133
(317) 232-9010
http://www.doe.state.in.us

Department of Education
Room 229, State House
Indianapolis, IN 46204-2798
(317) 232-6665
http://www.doe.state.in.us

Iowa
Department of Education
Grimes State Office Bldg.
East 14th and Grand Streets
Des Moines, IA 50319-0147
(515) 281-3245
http://www.state.ia.us/educate

Kansas
Department of Education
Kansas State Education Bldg.
120 East 10th Street
Topeka, KS 66612-1182
(785) 296-2288
http://www.ksbe.state.ks.us

Kentucky
Department of Education
18th Floor-Capital Plaza Tower
500 Mero Street
Frankfort, KY 40601
(502) 564-4606
http://www.kde.state.ky.us

Louisiana
Department of Education
P.O. Box 94064
Baton Rouge, LA 70804-9064
(504) 342-3490
http://www.doe.state.la.us

Maine
Department of Education
State House Station 23
Augusta, ME 04333
(207) 287-5944
http://www.state.me.us/
education/homepage.htm

Maryland
Department of Education
200 West Baltimore Street
Baltimore, MD 21201
(410) 333-2142
http://sailor.lib.md.us/msde

Massachusetts
Department of Education
350 Main Street
Malden, MA 02148
(781) 388-3300
http://info.doe.mass.edu

Michigan
Department of Education
P.O. Box 30008
Lansing, MI 48909
(517)373-3310
http://www.mde.state.mi.us

Minnesota
Department of Education
616 Capitol Square Bldg.
St. Paul, MN 55101

(612) 296-2046
http://www.educ.state.mn.us

Mississippi
Department of Education
Box 771
550 High Street
Jackson, MS 39205-0771
(601) 359-3483
http://mdek12.state.ms.us

Missouri
Department of Elementary and
Secondary Education
P.O. Box 480
205 Jefferson Street
Jefferson City, MO 65102
(573) 751-0051
http://services.dese.state.mo.us

Montana
Office of Public Instruction
P.O. Box 202501
106 State Capitol
Helena, MT 59620-2501
(406) 444-3150
http://161.7.114.15/OPI/OPIHTML

Nebraska
Department of Education
301 Centennial Mall South
Box 94987
Lincoln, NE 68509-4987
(800) 371-4642
http://www.NDE.State.NE.US

Nevada
Department of Education
1850 E. Sahara, Suite 200
Las Vegas, NV 89158
(702) 386-5401
fsouth@nsn.k12.unr.edu (email only
for Nevada)

New Hampshire
Department of Education
101 Pleasant Street
State Office Park South
Concord, NH 03301
(603) 271-2407
http://www.state.nh.us/doe/
education.html

New Jersey
Department of Education
CN 503

Trenton, NJ 08625-0503
(609) 292-2070
http://www.state.nj.us/education

New Mexico
Department of Education
Education Building
300 Don Gaspar
Santa Fe, NM 87501-2786
(505) 827-6587
http://sde.state.nm.us

New York
Office of Teaching
Room 5A11-CEC
State Education Department
Albany, NY 12230
(518) 474-3901
http://www.nysed.gov

North Carolina
Department of Public Instruction
301 North Wilmington Street
Raleigh, NC 27601-2825
(919) 733-4125
http://www.dpi.state.nc.us

North Dakota
Department of Public Instruction
State Capitol Building, 11th Floor
600 Boulevard Avenue East
Bismarck, ND 58505-0440
(701) 224-2264
http://www.sendit.nodak.edu/dpi

Northern Mariana Islands
Department of Education
Commonwealth of the Northern
Mariana Islands
P.O. Box 1370 CK
Saipan, MP 96950
(OS) 670-322-6451
none

Ohio
Department of Education
65 South Front Street, Room 1012
Columbus, OH 43266-0308
(614) 466-3593
http://www.ode.ohio.gov

Oklahoma
Professional Standards
Department of Education

Oliver Hodge Memorial Education
Building
2500 North Lincoln Boulevard,
Room 211
Oklahoma City, OK 73105-4599
(405) 521-3337
http://sde.state.ok.us

Oregon
Teacher Standards and Practices
Commission
630 Center Street, N.E., Suite 200
Salem, OR 97310
(503) 378-3586
http://www/ode.state.or.us

Department of Education
700 Pringle Parkway, S.E.
Salem, OR 97310-0290
(503) 378-3573
http://www/ode.state.or.us

Pennsylvania
Department of Education
333 Market Street, 10th Floor
Harrisburg, PA 17126-0333
(717) 787-2967
http://www/cas.psu.edu/pde.html

Puerto Rico
Department of Education
P.O. Box 759
Hato Rey, PR 00919
(809) 751-5372
none

Rhode Island
Department of Education
22 Hayes Street
Providence, RI 02908
(401) 277-2675
http://instruct.ride.ri.net/ride home
page.html

South Carolina
Department of Education
10006 Rutledge Building
1429 Senate Street
Columbia, SC 29201
(803) 734-8492
http://www.state.sc.us/sde

Office of Education Professions
Teacher Certification Section
1015 Rutledge Building

Columbia, SC 29201
(803) 774-8466
http://www.state.sc.us/sde

South Dakota
Teacher Education & Certification
Department of Education
700 Governors Drive
Pierre, SD 57501-2291
(605) 773-3553
http://www.state.sd.us/state/
executive/deca/

Tennessee
Department of Education
100 Cordell Hull Building
Nashville, TN 37243-0375
(615) 741-2731
http://www.state.tn.us/other/sde/
homepage.htm

Office of Teacher Licensing
710 James Robertson Parkway
5th Floor, Gateway Plaza
Nashville, TN 37243-0377
(615) 741-1644
http://www.state.tn.us/other/sde/
homepage.htm

Texas
Texas Education Agency
William B. Travis Building
1701 North Congress Avenue
Austin, TX 78701-1494
(512) 463-8976
http://www.tea.texas.gov

Utah
Office of Education
250 East 500 South Street
Salt Lake City, UT 84111
(801) 538-7740
http://www.usoe.k12.ut.us

Vermont
Department of Education
120 State Street
Montpelier, VT 05602-2703
(802) 828-2445
http://www.state.vt.us/educ

Virgin Islands
Department of Education
44-46 Kogens Gade
Charlotte Amalie, VI 00802

(809) 774-2810
none

Virginia
Department of Education
James Monroe Building
Fourteenth and Franklin Streets
P.O. Box 6-Q
Richmond, VA 23216-2120
(804) 225-2755
http://www.pen.k12.va.us/go/
VDOE

Office of Professional Licensure
Department of Education
P.O. Box 2120
Richmond VA 23216-2120
(804) 225-2022
http://www.pen.k12.va.us/go/
VDOE

Washington
Department of Public Instruction
Old Capitol Building
P.O. Box 47200
Olympia, WA 98504-7200
(206) 753-6773
http://www.ospi.wednet.edu

West Virginia
Department of Education
Building 6, Room 337
1900 Kanawha Blvd., East
Charleston, WV 25305-0330
(800) 982-2378
http://access.k12.wv.us

Wisconsin
Teacher Education, Licensing and
Placement
Department of Public Instruction

Box 7841
125 South Webster Street
Madison, WI 53707-7841
(608) 266-1027
http://badger.state.wi.us/agencies/
dpi

Wyoming
Department of Education
2300 Capitol Avenue
Hathaway Building, 2nd Floor
Cheyenne, WY 82002
(307) 777-7291
http://www.k12.wy.us/
wdehome.html

U.S. Department of Education
www.ed.gov

Canadian Education Agencies

Employment & Immigration
Canada
Public Inquiries Centre
Public Affairs Branch
140 Promenade du Portage,
Phase IV
Hull PQ K1A OJ9
(819) 994-6313

Statistics Canada
Statistical Reference Centre (NCR)
Ottawa, ON K1A OT6
(613) 951-8116

Alta.: Alberta Education
Communications Branch
Devonian Bldg.
11160 Jasper Ave., 2nd Floor
Edmonton, AB T5K OL2
(403) 427-2285

Alberta Advanced Education &
Career Development
City Centre
10155 - 102 St., 7th Floor
Edmonton, AB T5J 4L5
(403) 422-4495

B.C.: Ministry of Education #325
620 Superior Street
Victoria, BC V8V 1X4
(604) 356-2500

Man.: Manitoba Education &
Training #221
1200 Portage Avenue
Winnipeg, MB R3G OT5
(204) 945-6176

N.B.: Department of Education
P.O. Box 6000
Fredericton, NB E3B 5H1
(506) 453-3678

Nfld.: Department of Education
Information Officer
Confederation Building
P.O. Box 8700
St. John's, NF A1B 4J6
(709) 729-5097

N.S.: Department of Education,
Publication & Communication
P.O. Box 578
Trade Mart
Halifax, NS B3J 2S9
(902) 424-5570

Ont.: Ministry of Education &
Training,
Communications & Marketing
Branch
Mowat Block
900 Bay Street, 14th Floor
Toronto, ON M7A 1L2
(416) 325-2929

Toll Free: 1-800-387-5514
TDD: 1-800-263-2892

P.E.I.: Department of Education &
Human Resources
P.O. Box 2000
Charlottetown, PE C1A 7N8
(902) 368-4600

Que.: Ministere del'Education,
Direction
des communications, 11e etage
1035 De La Chevrotiere
Quebec, PQ G1R 5A5
(418) 643-7095

Sask.: Saskatchewan Education,
Training & Employment, Inquiries
2220 College Avenue
Regina, SK S4P 3V7
(306) 787-6030

N.W.T.: Department of Education
Culture & Employment
P.O. Box 1320
Yellowknife, NT X1A 2L9
(403) 873-7529

Yukon: Yukon Education
P.O. Box 2703
Whitehorse, YT Y1A 2C6
(403) 667-5141

Directory of Chief State School Offices

Alabama
Superintendent of Education
State Department of Education
Gordon Persons Office Building
50 North Ripley St
Montgomery, AL 36130-3901
(205) 242-9700
Term of office: Appointed by the state board of education for a four-year term.

Alaska
Commissioner of Education
State Department of Education
Alaska State Office Building
Pouch F
Juneau, AK 99811
(907) 465-2800
Term of office: Appointed by the state board of education with the concurrence of the governor and serving at the will of the board.

Arizona
Superintendent of Public Instruction
State Department of Education
1535 W. Jefferson St.
Phoenix, AZ 85007
(602) 542-4361
Term of office: Elected by popular vote for a four-year term.

Arkansas
Director, General Education Division

State Department of Education
Four State Capitol Mall, Room 304A
Little Rock, AR 72201-1071
(501) 682-4204
Term of office: Appointed by the state board of education and serving at the will of the governor.

California
Superintendent of Public Instruction
State Department of Education
721 Capitol Mall
Sacramento, CA 95814
(916) 657-5485

Colorado
Commissioner of Education
State Department of Education
201 East Colfax Ave.
Denver, CO 80203-1706
(303) 866-8805
Term of office: Appointed by the state board of education and serving at the will of the board.

Connecticut
Commissioner of Education
State Department of Education
165 Capitol Ave.
Room 305, State Office Building
Hartford, CT 06106
(860) 566-5061
Term of office: Appointed by the state board of education and confirmed by the governor.

Delaware
Superintendent of Public Instruction
State Department of Public Instruction
P.O. Box 1402 Townsend Building, #279
Federal and Locherman Sts.
Dover, DE 19903
(302) 739-4601
Term of office: Appointed by the state board of education and serving at the will of the board.

District of Columbia
Superintendent of Public Schools
District of Columbia Public Schools
415 12th St., NW
Washington, D.C. 20004
(202) 724-4222
Term of office: Appointed by the school board for a three-year term.

Florida
Commissioner of Education
State Department of Education
Capitol Building, Room PL 08
Tallahassee, FL 32301
(904) 487-1785
Term of office: Elected by popular vote for a four-year term.

Georgia
Superintendent of Schools
State Department of Education
2066 Twin Towers East

Reprinted with permission from *Education Week*, Vol. 12, No. 23, March 3, 1993.

205 Butler St.
Atlanta, GA 30334
(404) 656-2800
Term of office: Elected by popular
vote for a four-year term.

Hawaii
Superintendent of Education
Department of Education
1390 Miller St., #307
Honolulu, HI 96804
(808) 586-3230
Term of office: Appointed by the
state board of education and
serving at the will of the board.

Idaho
Superintendent of Public
Instruction
State Department of Education
Len B. Jordan Office Building
650 West State St.
Boise, ID 83720
(208) 334-3300
Term of office: Elected by popular
vote for a four-year term.

Illinois
Superintendent of Education
State Department of Education
100 North First St.
Springfield, IL 62777
(217) 782-2221
Term of office: Appointed by the
state board of education and
serving at the will of the board.

Indiana
Superintendent of Public
Instruction
State Department of Education
State House, Room 229
Indianapolis, IN 46204-2798
(317) 232-6665
Term of office: Elected by popular
vote for a four-year-term.

Iowa
Director of Education
State Department of Education
Grimes State Office Building
East 14th and Grand Sts.
Des Moines, IA 50319-0146
(515) 281-5294

Term of office: Appointed by the
governor and serving at the will of
the governor.

Kansas
Commissioner of Education
State Department of Education
120 South East 10th St.
Topeka, KS 66612
(785) 296-3202
Term of office: Appointed by the
state board of education and
serving at the will of the board.

Kentucky
Commissioner of Education
State Department of Education
Capitol Plaza Tower
500 Metro St.
Frankfort, KY 40601
(502) 564-3141
Term of office: Serving under a
contract with the state board of
education.

Louisiana
Superintendent of Education
State Department of Education
626 North Fourth St.
P.O. Box 94064
Baton Rouge, LA 70804-9064
(504) 342-3602
Term of office: Appointed by the
state board of secondary and
elementary education.

Maine
Commissioner of Education
Maine Department of Education
State House Station 23
Augusta, ME 04333
(207) 287-5114
Term of office: Appointed by the
governor for a four-year term, and
serving a term concurrent with that
of the governor.

Maryland
Superintendent of Schools
State Department of Education
200 West Baltimore St.
Baltimore, MD 21201
(410) 333-2200

Term of office: Appointed by the
state board of education for a four-
year term.

Massachusetts
Commissioner of Education
State Department of Education
Quincy Center Plaza
1385 Hancock St.
Quincy, MA 02169
(781) 388-3300
Term of office: Appointed by the
state board and serving at the will
of the board.

Michigan
Superintendent of Public
Instruction
State Department of Education
P.O. Box 30008
608 West Allegan St.
Lansing, MI 48909
(517) 373-3354
Term of office: Appointed by the
state board of education for a three-
year term.

Minnesota
Commissioner of Education
State Department of Education
712 Capitol Square Building
550 Cedar St.
St. Paul, MN 55101
(612) 296-2358
Term of office: Appointed by the
governor for a four-year term
concurrent with that of the
governor.

Mississippi
Superintendent of Education
State Department of Education
P.O. Box 771
550 High St., Room 501
Jackson, MS 39205-0771
(601) 359-3513
Term of office: Appointed to the
position by the board of education.

Missouri
Commissioner of Education
Department of Elementary and
Secondary Education
P.O. Box 480
205 Jefferson St., 6th Floor

Jefferson City, MO 65102
(573) 751-4446
Term of office: Appointed by the state board of education and serving at the will of the board.

Montana
Superintendent of Public Instruction
State Office of Public Instruction
106 State Capitol
Helena, MT 59620
(406) 444-3680
Term of office: Elected by popular vote for a four-year term.

Nebraska
Commissioner of Education
State Department of Education
P.O. Box 94967
301 Centennial Mall, South
Lincoln, NE 68509
(402) 471-5020
Term of office: Appointed by the state board of education with a three-year contract.

Nevada
Superintendent of Public Instruction
State Department of Education
400 West King St.
Capitol Complex
Carson City, NV 89710
(702) 687-3100
Term of office: Appointed by the state board of education and serving at the discretion of the board.

New Hampshire
Commissioner of Education
State Department of Education
101 Pleasant St.
State Office Park South
Concord, NH 03301
(603) 271-3144
Term of office: Appointed by the state board of education and serving at the discretion of the board.

New Jersey
Commissioner of Education
State Department of Education

225 West State St. CN 500
Trenton, NJ 08625-0500
(609) 292-4450
Term of office: Appointed by the governor with state Senate approval.

New Mexico
Superintendent of Public Instruction
State Department of Education Building
300 Don Gasper
Santa Fe, NM 87501-2786
(505) 827-8516
Term of office: Appointed by the state board of education and serving at the discretion of the board.

New York
Commissioner of Education
State Education Department
111 Education Building
Washington Ave.
Albany, NY 12234
(518) 474-5844
Term of office: Appointed by the board of regents and serving at the discretion of the board.

North Carolina
Superintendent of Public Instruction
State Department of Public Instruction
Education Building, Room 194
116 West Edenton St.
Raleigh, NC 27603-1712
(919) 733-3813
Term of office: Elected by popular vote for a four-year term.

North Dakota
Superintendent of Public Instruction
State Department of Public Instruction
State Capitol Building 11th Floor
600 Boulevard Ave. East
Bismarck, ND 58505-0440
(701) 224-2261
Term of office: Elected by popular vote for a four-year term.

Ohio
Superintendent of Public Instruction
State Department of Education
65 South Front St., Room 808
Columbus, OH 43266-0308
(614) 466-3304
Term of office: Appointed by the state board of education and serving at the discretion of the board.

Oklahoma
Superintendent of Public Instruction
Secretary of Education
State Department of Education
Oliver Hodge Memorial Education Building
2500 North Lincoln Blvd.
Oklahoma City, OK 73105-4599
(405) 521-3301
Term of office: Elected by popular vote for a four-year term.

Oregon
Superintendent of Public Instruction
State Department of Education
700 Pringle Parkway, S.E.
Salem, OR 97310
(503) 378-3573
Term of office: Elected by popular vote for a four-year term.

Pennsylvania
Secretary of Education
State Department of Education
333 Market St., 10th Floor
Harrisburg, PA 17126-0333
(717) 787-5820
Term of office: Appointed by the governor and serving at the discretion of the governor.

Rhode Island
Commissioner of Education
State Department of Education
22 Hayes St.
Providence, RI 02908
(401) 277-2031
Term of office: Appointed by the state board of education and serving at the discretion of the board.

South Carolina
Superintendent of Education
State Department of Education
1006 Rutledge Building
1429 Senate St.
Columbia, SC 29201
(803) 734-8492
Term of office: Elected by popular
vote for a four-year term.

South Dakota
Secretary of Education
Department of Education and
Cultural Affairs
700 Governors Dr.
Pierre, SD 57501
(605) 773-3134
Term of office: Appointed by the
state board of education and
serving at the discretion of the
governor.

Tennessee
Commissioner of Education
State Department of Education
100 Cordell Hull Building
Nashville, TN 37219
(615) 741-2731
Term of office: Appointed by the
governor and serving concurrently
with the governor's term.

Texas
Commissioner of Education
Texas Education Agency
William B. Travis Building
1701 North Congress Ave.
Austin, TX 78701-1494
(512) 463-8985
Term of office: Appointed by the
state board of education for a four-
year term.

Utah
Superintendent of Public
Instruction
State Office of Education
250 East 500 South
Salt Lake City, UT 84111
(801) 538-7510
Term of office: Appointed by the
state board of education with
approval of the governor and
serving at the board's discretion.

Vermont
Commissioner of Education
State Department of Education
120 State St.
Montpelier, VT 05602-2703
(802) 828-3135
Term of office: Appointed by the
state board of education, with
approval of the governor, and
serving at the board's discretion.

Virginia
Superintendent of Public
Instruction
State Department of Education
James Monroe Building
14th and Franklin Streets
Richmond, VA 23216-2060
(804) 225-2023
Term of office: Appointed by the
governor and confirmed by the
General Assembly for four years
concurrent with the governor's
term.

Washington
Superintendent of Public
Instruction
State Department of Public
Instruction

Old Capitol Building, Washington
& Legion
P.O. Box 47200
Olympia, WA 98504
(208) 506-6904
Term of office: Elected by popular
vote for a four-year term.

West Virginia
Superintendent of Schools
State Department of Education
1900 Kanawha Blvd., East
Building 6 Room B-358
Charleston, WV 25305
(304) 558-2081
Term of office: Appointed by the
state board of education and
serving at the discretion of the
board.

Wisconsin
Superintendent of Public
Instruction
State Department of Public
Instruction
125 South Webster St.
Post Office Box 7841
Madison, WI 53707
(608) 266-1771
Term of office: Elected by popular
vote for a four-year term.

Wyoming
Superintendent of Public
Instruction
State Department of Education
2300 Capitol Avenue, 2nd Floor
Hathaway Building
Cheyenne, WY 82002-0060
(302) 777-7675
Term of office: Elected by popular
vote for a four-year term.

Source: Council of Chief State School Officers.

Methods of Selecting Chief State School Officers

	Appointed by State Board of Education	Appointed by Governor	Elected by People
Alabama	X		
Alaska	X		
Arizona			X
Arkansas	X		
California			X
Colorado	X		
Connecticut	X		
Delaware	X		
Florida			X
Georgia			X
Hawaii	X		
Idaho			X
Illinois	X		
Indiana			X
Iowa		X	
Kansas	X		
Kentucky	X		
Louisiana	X		
Maine		X	
Maryland	X		
Massachusetts	X		

Source: National Association of State Boards of Education.

	Appointed by State Board of Education	Appointed by Governor	Elected by People
Michigan	X		
Minnesota		X	
Mississippi	X		
Missouri	X		
Montana			X
Nebraska	X		
Nevada	X		
New Hampshire	X		
New Jersey		X	
New Mexico	X		
New York	X		
North Carolina			X
North Dakota			X
Ohio	X		
Oklahoma			X
Oregon			X
Pennsylvania		X	
Rhode Island	X		
South Carolina			X
South Dakota	X		
Tennessee		X	
Texas		X	
Utah	X		
Vermont	X		
Virginia		X	
Washington			X
West Virginia	X		
Wisconsin			X
Wyoming			X
District of Columbia	X		

Methods of Selecting State School Board Members

	Elected by People or Representatives	Appointed by Governor	Other
Alabama	X		
Alaska		X	
Arizona	X		
Arkansas		X	
California		X	
Colorado	X		
Connecticut		X	
Delaware		X	
Florida	X		
Georgia		X	
Hawaii	X		
Idaho		X	
Illinois		X	
Indiana		X	
Iowa		X	
Kansas	X		
Kentucky		X	
Louisiana			X
Maine		X	
Maryland		X	
Massachusetts		X	

Source: National Association of State Boards of Education.

(continued on next page)

Source: National Association of State Boards of Education.

	Elected by People or Representatives	Appointed by Governor	Other
Michigan	X		
Minnesota		X	
Mississippi			X
Missouri		X	
Montana		X	
Nebraska	X		
Nevada	X		
New Hampshire		X	
New Jersey		X	
New Mexico			X
New York	X		
North Carolina		X	
North Dakota		X	
Ohio	X		
Oklahoma		X	
Oregon		X	
Pennsylvania		X	
Rhode Island		X	
South Carolina	X		
South Dakota		X	
Tennessee		X	
Texas	X		
Utah	X		
Vermont		X	
Virginia		X	
Washington	X		
West Virginia		X	
Wisconsin	(NO BOARD)		
Wyoming		X	
District of Columbia	X		

52

Computer Companies

Apple Computer, Inc.
20525 Mariani Avenue
Cupertino, CA 95014
(408) 996-1010

AST Computer
16215 Alton Parkway
Irvine, CA 92619-7005
(714) 727-4141

AT&T Co. Communications Group
295 N. Maple Ave.
Basking Ridge, NJ 07920
(201) 221-8851

Compaq Computer Corporation
P.O. Box 692000
Houston, TX 77269-2000
(713) 370-0670

Dell Computer Corporation
9505 Arboretum Blvd.
Austin, TX 78759-7299
(512) 728-8797

Digital Equipment Corp.
146 Main St.

Maynard, MA 01754
(617) 897-1111

Gateway 2000 Computers
610 Gateway Drive
N. Sioux City, SD 57049-2000
(605) 232-2222

Hewlett-Packard
3000 Hanover St.
Palo Alto, CA 94304
(415) 857-1501

IBM Corporation
Old Orchard Road
Armonk, NY 10504
(914) 765-1900

Leading Edge
117 Flanders Road
West Borough, MA 01581
(508) 836-4800

NEC Technologies
1414 Massachusetts Ave.
Boxboro, MA 01719
(508) 264-8000

Packard Bell
31717 La Tienda Drive
West Lake Village, CA 91362
(818) 865-1555

Panasonic Computer Products
Two Panasonic Way 76-0
Secaucus, NJ 07094
(201) 392-4500

Tandy Corporation/Radio Shack
Dept. 88-A-530
300 One Tandy Center
Fort Worth, TX 76102
(817) 390-3011

Texas Instruments, Inc.
Data Systems Group
P.O. Box 809063, DSG-163
Dallas, TX 75380
(800) 527-3500

Zenith Data Systems Corporation
2150 E. Lake Cook Rd.
Buffalo Grove, IL 60089
(708) 808-5000

Source: John H. Johansen, et al., *American Education: An Introduction to Teaching,* 7th ed. 1993. Dubuque, Iowa: Times Mirror Higher Education Group, Inc.

Educational Software Companies from A-to-Z

The following list of companies is but a small sample of the over 1,000 educational software companies listed by the PEP Registry on the World Wide Web.

Academic Software, Inc.
331 W. 2nd St.
Lexington, KY 40507
10800-842-2357
www.acsw.com

Advantage Learning Systems, Inc.
P.O. Box 8036
Wisconsin Rapids, WI 54495
1-800-338-4204
www.advlearn.com

Afrolink Software
P.O. Box 36708
Los Angeles CA 90036-0708
(213) 731-5465
www.trip.com/~griotech/
blistmac.htm

Barnum Software
3450 Lack Shore Ave, Suite 200A
Oakland, Ca 94610
1-800-553-9155
www.thequartermile.com

Broderbund Software
PO Box 6125
Novato, CA 94948-6125
800-548-1798
Educational Support Line
800-474-8840
www.broderbund.com/

Cognitive Technologies
Corporation
5009 Cloister Dr.
Rockville, MD 20852
1-800-335-0781
www.cogtech.com

COMPAQ
P.O. Box 692000
Houston, TX 77269-2000
281-370-0670
www.compaq.com

DiscoverWare Inc.
Fifth Floor, 926 5th Ave. SW
Calgary, Alberta
Canada T2P 0N7
403.237.0426
1.800.465.3641
www.discoverware.com

Educational Software Products
Kate Lockner & Sales Inquiries—
ESP
299 Tanager Court
Deerfield, IL 60015
1-888-377-3776
www.expexpert.com

Expert Software, Inc.
800 Douglas Road
Executive Tower
Coral Gables, Florida 33134-3160

(305) 567-9990
www.expertsoftware.com

Falcon Software, Inc.
One Hollis Street
Wellesley, MA 02181 USA
Phone (781) 235-1767
www.falconsoftware.com

Gryphon Software Corporation
7220 Trade Street
San Diego, CA 92121 USA
(619) 536-8815
Product Orders: (888) 8GRYPHON
World Wide Web:
http://www.gryphonsw.com/

Girl Tech., Inc.
Public Relations
PO Box 4062
San Rafael, CA
93913-4062
(415) 256-1510
www.girltech.com

Harcourt Brace & Company
Order Fulfillment Department
6277 Sea Harbor Drive
Orlando, FL 32887
Toll Free: 1-800-225-5425
www.hbschool.com

Source: PEP Registry of Educational Software Publishers PEP: Resources for Parents, Educators & Publishers http://www.microweb.com/pepsite/Software/publishers.html

Houghton Mifflin
1900 S. Batavia Avenue
Geneva, IL 60134-3399
(800) 733-2828
www.eduplace.com

Info Math
1-888-MATH-456
www.infomath.com

IBM K-12 Education
1-800-IBM-4EDU
www.solutions.ibm.com/K12

Jon Noonan Educational Software
Box 427
Mira Loma, CA
USA 91752-0427
909-360-5944
www.pe.net/~jnes

Jostens Learning Corporation
9920 Pacific Heights Blvd.
San Diego, CA 92121
800-521-8538
www.jlc.com

K12 Micromedia Publishing
16 Mckee Dr.
Mahwah, NJ 07430
800-292-1997
www.k12mmp.com

KnowWonder, Inc
1-888-KNOWNDR (566-9637)
www.knowwonder.com

Knowledge Revolution
66 Bovet Road, Suite 200
San Mateo, CA 94402
800-766-6615
www.krev.com

The Learning Box
4508 Valleycrest Dr.
Arlington, TX 76013
800-743-9450
www.learningbox.com

The Learning Company, Inc.
One Athenaeum Street
Cambridge, MA 02477
617-494-1200
www.learningco.com

MathMedia Educational Software,
Inc.
3100 Dundee Road, Suite 703
Northbrook Illinois 60062
1-888-FOR-MATH
www.mathmedia.com

McGraw-Hill School Division
Corporate Headquarters
1221 Avenue of the Americas
New York, NY 10020
(212) 512-2000
www.mmhschool.com

Microsoft
10700 Northrup Way
Box 97200
Bellevue, WA 98009
(206) 828-8080
www.microsoft.com

NECTAR Foundation
10 Bowhill Ave.
Nepean, Ontario
Canada K2E6S7
613-224-3031
http://spdcs.crcssb.edu.on.ca/
nectar

Nordic Software
(800)-306-6502
www.nordiscsoftware.com

OnScreen Science, Inc.
46 Wallace St., Suite 20
Somerville, MA 02144
(800) 617-6416
www.onscreen-sci.com

Oryx Press
P.O. Box 33889
Phoenix, Arizona 85067-3889
800-279-6799
www.oryxpress.com

Paper Trail Software
P.O. Box 36262
Las Vegas, NV 89133
Voice Mail or Fax: 702-656-1950
http://www.tcd.net/~papertrl/

Point Software
P.O. Box 710
St. Petersburg, Florida 33731
(813) 896-7711
www.netizard.com

Queue, Inc.
338 Commerce Drive
Fairfield, CT 06432
203-335-0906
800-232-2224
www.queueinc.com

RJ Cooper & Associates
24843 Del Prado #283
DanaPoint, CA 92629
800-RJCooper
www.rjcooper.com

Scholastic Order Processing
2931 East McCarty Street
Jefferson City, MO 65101
800-223-4011
www.scholastic.com

Science Education Softward Inc.
(SESI)
PO Box 60790
Palo Alto, CA 94306
415-367-6457 (voice) 415-366-2744
(fax)
www.hungryfrog.com

Tom Snyder Productions
80 Coolidge Hill Road
Watertown, MA 02172
1-800-342-0236
www.techtsp.com

TeacherSoft, Inc.
903 East 18th Street, 2nd Floor
Plano, TX 75074
972-424-7882
www.teachersoft.com

Texas Learning Technology Group
Attn: Cathy Austin
P.O. Box 2947
Austin, Texas 78768-2947
1-800-580-8584, ext. 6101
www.tasb.org

Universal Learning Technology
39 Cross Street
Peabody, MA 01960
(508) 538-0036
www.cast.org

Ventura Educational Systems
P.O. Box 425
910 Ramona Avenue–Suite E

Grover Beach, Ca 93433
800-336-1022
www.venturaaes.com

Visions Technology in Education
710 N.E. Cleveland Ave.
Gresham, OR 97030 Suite 130
800-877-0858
www.visteched.com

Weaver Instructional Systems, Inc.
6161 28th Street SE
Grand Rapids, MI 49546
800-634-8916
www.wisesoft.com

WorldSoft Technical Services

775 N 1570 W
Pleasant Grove, UT 84062
(801) 796-3822 voice
www.worldsoft.com

Xavier Educational Software Ltd.
Department of Psychology
University of Wales Bangor
Gwynedd. UK. LL57 2DG.
Tel: +44 (0) 1248 382616
www.psych.bangor.ac.uk/
deptpsych/xavier/xavier.html

Xlsoft International
12K Mauchly
Irvine, CA 92618
Tel: 714-453-2781

www.xisoft.com

Yale University Press
Order Department
PO Box 209040
New Haven, CT 06520
800-987-7323
www.yale.edu

Zimgraphics, Lts.
26 Scollard Street
Toronto, Ontario, Canada M5R 1E9
(416) 929-8155, Sales—
(800) 929-8155
http://www.netusa.com/pcsoft/
library/p_1028.htm

Resources
and Hotlines

AIDS Action Council & Foundation . . . . (202) 986-1300
AIDS Clinical Trials Information Service . . . . (800) 874-2572
AIDS Helpline (Health Professionals) . . . . (800) 548-4659
Al-Anon & Alateen . . . . (800) 356-9996
Alcoholics Anonymous. . . . . (800) 452-7990
American Foundation for AIDS Research (AmFar) . . . . (212) 682-7440
American Red Cross (AIDS Education) . . . . (703) 206-7180
American Suicide Foundation . . . . (800) 531-4477
Ask A Nurse . . . . (800) 535-1111
Boys Town. . . . . (800) 448-3000
Bureau of Indian Affairs, Child Abuse Hotline. . . . . (800) 633-5155
Child Find of America. . . . . (800) 426-5678
Child Help USA National Child Abuse Hotline . . . . (800) 422-4453
Child Quest International Sighting Line . . . . (800) 248-8020
Children's Rights of America. . . . . (800) 442-4673
Crisis Nursery & Respite Referral . . . . (800) 473-1727
Families Anonymous. . . . . (800) 736-9805
Literacy Hotline/Department of Education . . . . (800) 228-8813
Names Project. . . . . (415) 882-5500
National AIDS Hotline . . . . (800) 342-2437
National AIDS Hotline (Hearing Impaired) . . . . (800) 243-7889
National AIDS Information Clearinghouse . . . . (800) 458-5231
National AIDS Program Office . . . . (202) 690-5471
National Center for Missing & Exploited Children . . . . (800) 843-5678
National Clearinghouse for Alcohol & Drug Info. . . . . (800) 729-6686
National Coalition Against Domestic Violence. . . . . (303) 839-1852
National Cocaine Hotline . . . . (800) 262-2463
National Council on Alcoholism and Chemical Dependency Hope Line. . . . . . . (800) 622-2255
National Criminal Justice Reference Service . . . . (301) 251-5500
National Family Planning & Reproductive Health Organization . . . . (202) 563-7742
National Foundation for Cancer Research. . . . . (800) 321-2873
National Health Information Center. . . . . (800) 336-4797
National Institute on Drug Abuse Hotline. . . . . (800) 662-4357
National Mental Health Association. . . . . (800) 433-5959
Office of Minority Health Resource Center . . . . (800) 444-6472
National Pediatric HIV Resource Center . . . . (800) 362-0071
National Referral Network for Kids in Crisis . . . . (800) 543-7283
National Runaway Hotline. . . . . (800) 621-4000

Parents Anonymous . . . . (909) 621-6184
Pediatric AIDS Coalition. . . . . (800) 336-5475
Planned Parenthood Federation of America . . . . (800) 829-7732
Social Security Administration . . . . (800) 772-1213
STD National Hotline . . . . (800) 227-8922
Step Family Foundation, The . . . . (212) 799-7837

National Service Organizations

Action for Child Protection
4724C Park Rd.
Charlotte, NC 28209
(704) 529-1080
(704) 529-1132 FAX

AIDS Clinical Trials Information
Service (ACTIS)
P.O. Box 6421
Rockville, MD 20849-6421
(800) 874-2572
(800) 243-7012 Deaf Access (TTY)
(301) 217-0023 International Line
(301) 738-6616 FAX

American Academy of Child &
Adolescent Psychiatry
3615 Wisconsin Ave., N.W.
Washington, D.C. 20016
(800) 333-7636
(202) 966-2891 FAX

American Association for Marriage
& Family Therapy
1100 17th Street, N.W., 10th Floor
Washington, D.C. 20036
(202) 452-0109
(202) 223-2329 FAX

American Association on Mental
Retardation
444 North Capitol St., N.W., Suite
846
Washington, D.C. 20001-1512
(800) 424-3688
(202) 387-2193 FAX

American Association of School
Administrators
1801 North Moore Street
Arlington, VA 22209-9988
(703) 528-0700
(703) 841-1543 FAX

American Bar Association
750 North Lake Shore Dr.
Chicago, IL 60611
(800) 621-6159
Family Law Section
(312) 988-5613
(312) 988-6281 FAX

American Bar Association Center
on Children & the Law
1800 M. Street, N.W., Suite S-200
Washington, D.C. 20036
(212) 331-2250

American College of Nurse-
Midwives
818 Connecticut Ave., N.W., Suite
900
Washington, D.C. 20006
(202) 728-9860
(202) 728-9897 FAX

American Foundation for AIDS
Research (AmFAR)
733 Third Ave., 12th Floor
New York, NY 10017
(212) 682-7440
(212) 682-9812 FAX

American Foundation for the Blind
(AFB)
11 Penn Plaza, Suite 300
New York, NY 10001
(800) 232-5463
(212) 620-2158 TDD
(212) 727-7418 FAX

American Home Economics
Association
1555 King Street
Alexandria, VA 22314
(703) 706-4600
(703)706-4663 FAX

American Humane Association -
Children's Division
63 Inverness Drive East
Englewood, CO 80112-5117
(800) 227-4645
(303) 792-5333 FAX

American National Red Cross
430 17th Street, N.W.
Washington, D.C. 20006
(202) 737-8300
(202) 639-3000 FAX

American Nurses Association
600 Maryland Ave., S.W., Suite 100
West
Washington, D.C. 20024-4444
(202) 554-4444
(202) 554-2262 FAX

American Occupational Therapy
Association (AOTA)
4720 Montgomery Lane -
P.O. Box 31220
Bethesda, MD 20284-1220
(301) 652-2682
(800) 377-8555 TDD
(301) 948-5512 FAX

American Professional Society on
the Abuse of Children
407 S. Dearborn, Suite 1300
Chicago, IL 60605
(312) 554-0166
(312) 554-0919 FAX

American Psychological
Association
750 1st Street, N.E.
Washington, D.C. 20002
(800) 374-2721
(202) 336-6069 FAX

American Public Health Association
1015 15th Street, N.W., Suite 300
Washington, D.C. 20005
(202) 789-5600
(202) 789-5661 FAX

American Public Welfare
Association
810 1st Street, N.E., Suite 500
Washington, D.C. 20002-4267
(202) 682-0100
(202) 289-6555 FAX

American Social Health Association
P.O. Box 13827
Research Triangle Park, NC 27709
(919) 361-8400
(919) 361-8425 FAX

American Society for Adolescent
Psychiatry
4330 East West Highway, Suite 1117
Bethesda, MD 20814-4408
(301) 718-6502
(301) 656-0989 FAX

American Speech-Language-
Hearing Association (ASHA)
10801 Rockville Pike
Rockville, MD 20852
(800) 638-8255
(301) 571-0457 FAX

American Youth Work Center
1200 17th St., N.W. 4th Floor
Washington, D.C. 20036
(202) 785-0764
(202) 728-0657 FAX

Armed Services YMCA of the USA
6225 Brandon Ave., Suite 215
Springfield, VA 22150-2510
(703) 866-1260
(703) 866-9215 FAX

Association for the Advancement of
Rehabilitation Technology (RESNA)
1700 N. Moore St., Suite 1540
Arlington, VA 22200
(703) 524-6686
(703) 524-6630 FAX

Association on American Indian
Affairs, Inc.
245 5th Ave., Suite 1801
New York, NY 10016
(800) 895-2242
(212) 685-4692 FAX

Association for the Care of
Children's Health
7910 Woodmont Ave., Suite 300
Bethesda, MD 20814-3015
(301) 654-6549
(301) 986-4553 FAX

Association for Childhood
Education International
11501 Georgia Ave., Suite 315
Wheaton, MD 20902
(800) 423-3563

Association on Mental Retardation
(ARC)
P.O. Box 1047
Arlington, TX 76004
(817) 261-6003
(817) 277-0553 TDD

Association for Persons with Severe
Handicaps
(206) 361-8870

Autism Society of America
7910 Woodmont Ave., Suite 650
Bethesda, MD 20814
(800) 328-8476

Big Brothers/Big Sisters of America
230 North 13th Street
Philadelphia, PA 19107
(215) 567-7000
(215) 567-0394 FAX

Boys & Girls Clubs of America
1230 W. Peachtree Street
Atlanta, GA 30309
(404) 815-5700

Boy Scouts of America
P.O. Box 152079
1325 Walnut Hill Lane
Irving, TX 75015-2079
(214) 580-2000
(214) 580-2502 FAX

Boys Town National Research
Hospital
555 North 30th Street
Omaha, NE 68131
(402) 498-6511
(402) 498-6638 FAX

The Bureau of At Risk Youth
645 New York Ave.
Huntington, NY 11743
(800) 999-6884
(516) 673-4544 FAX

Business Responds to AIDS
Resource Services (BRTA)
P.O. Box 6003
Rockville, MD 20849
(800) 458-5231
(800) 243-7012 Deaf Access Line
(TDD)

Camp Fire Boys & Girls
4601 Madison Ave.
Kansas, City, MO 64112
(800) 669-6884
(816) 756-0258 FAX

The Annie E. Casey Foundation
701 St. Paul Street
Baltimore, MD 21202
(401) 547-6600

Catholic Charities USA
1731 King Street, Suite 200
Alexandria, VA 22314
(703) 549-1390
(703) 549-1656 FAX

Center for the Study of Social Policy
1250 Eye Street, N.W., Suite 503
Washington, D.C. 20005
(202) 371-1565
(202) 371-1472 FAX

Center for the Study of Youth Policy
University of PA
School of Social Work
4200 Pine Street, 2nd Floor
Philadelphia, PA 19104-4090
(215) 898-2229
(215) 573-2791 FAX

Child Find of America, Inc.
P.O. Box 277
New Paltz, NY 12561
(800) 426-5678
(914) 255-5706 FAX

CHILDHELP USA
6463 Independence Ave.
Woodland Hills, CA 91367
(818) 347-7280
(800) 422-4453 HOTLINE
(818) 593-3257 FAX

Child Quest International
1440 Koll Circle, Suite 103
San Jose, CA 95112
(408) 453-9601
(800) 248-8020 Sighting Line
(408) 453-1927 FAX

Children of Alcoholics Foundation
P.O. Box 4185
Grand Central Station
New York, NY 10163-4185
(800) 359-2623
(212) 754-0664 FAX

Children's Defense Fund
25 E. Street, N.W.
Washington, D.C. 20001
(800) 233-1200
(202) 662-3510 FAX

The Children's Foundation
725 15th Street, N.W., Suite 505
Washington, D.C. 20005
(202) 347-3300
(202) 347-3382 FAX

The Children's Health Fund
317 East 64th Street
New York, NY 10021
(212) 535-9400
(212) 535-7488 FAX

Children's Research Center
6409 Odana Road
Madison, WI 53719
(608) 274-8882
(608) 274-3151 FAX

Child Welfare Institute
1349 W. Peachtree Street, N.E.
Atlanta, GA 30309
(404) 876-1934
(404) 876-7949 FAX

Child Welfare League of America
(CWLA)
440 First Street, N.W., Suite 310
Washington, D.C. 20001-2085
(202) 638-2952
(202) 638-4004 FAX

Cities in Schools, Inc.
1199 N. Fairfax St., Suite 300
Alexandria, VA 22314
(703) 519-8999
(703) 519-7213 FAX

Council on Adoptable Children, Inc.
666 Broadway, Suite 820
New York, NY 10012
(212) 475-0222
(212) 475-1972 FAX

Council for Exceptional Children
1920 Association Drive
Reston, VA 22091
(800) 328-0272
(703) 264-9494 FAX

Council of Jewish Federations
730 Broadway
New York, NY 10003
(212) 475-5000
(212) 529-5842 FAX

Covenant House
346 West 17th Street
New York, NY 10011-5002
(212) 727-4000
(800) 999-9999 HOTLINE
(212) 989-9098 FAX

Devereux National Headquarters
Box 400
19 So. Waterloo Rd.
Devon, PA 19333
(610) 964-3000

Education Commission of the States
707 17th Street, Suite 2700
Denver, CO 80202-3427
(303) 299-3600
(303) 296-8332 FAX

Family Resource Coalition
200 South Michigan Avenue., 16th
Floor
Chicago, IL 60604
(312) 341-0900
(312) 341-9361 FAX

Family Service America, Inc.
11700 West Lake Park Drive
Milwaukee, WI 53224
(800) 221-2681
(414) 359-1074 FAX

Family Violence & Sexual Assault
Institute
1310 Clinic Drive
Tyler, TX 75701
(903) 595-6600
(903) 595-6799 FAX

Foundation for Hospice &
Homecare
519 C Street, N.E.
Washington, D.C. 20002
(202) 547-6586
(202) 546-8968 FAX

Giarretto Institute
232 East Gish Road
San Jose, CA 95112
(408) 453-7616
(408) 453-9064 FAX

Girls Incorporated
30 East 33rd St.
New York, NY 10016
(212) 689-3700
(212) 683-1253 FAX

Girl Scouts of the USA
420 5th Avenue
New York, NY 10018
(800) 223-0624
(212) 852-6514 FAX

Incest Survivors Resource Network
International
P.O. Box 7375
Las Cruces, NM 88006-7375
(505) 521-4260

Institute for Urban & Minority
Education
P.O. Box 40
Teachers College, Columbia
University
New York, NY 10027
(212) 678-3433

International Child Resource
Institute (ICRI)
1810 Hopkins
Berkeley, CA 94707
(510) 644-1000
(510) 525-4106 FAX

Joint Action in Community
Services, Inc. (JACS)
5225 Wisconsin Ave., N.W., Suite
404
Washington, D.C. 20015
(202) 537-0996

Robert F. Kennedy Memorial
1206 30th Street, N.W.
Washington, D.C. 20007
(202) 333-1880
(202) 333-4903 FAX

KidsPeace National Centers
5300 KidsPeace Drive
Orefield, PA 18069-9101
(800) 845-3123
(212) 799-8001 FAX

Learning Disabilities Association of
America
4156 Library Road
Pittsburgh, PA 15234
(412) 341-1515
(412) 344-0224 FAX

Mental Health Association National
Headquarters
1021 Prince Street
Alexandria, VA 22314-2971
(800) 969-6642
(703) 684-5968 FAX

Military Family Resource Center
4015 Wilson Blvd., Suite 903,
Tower 3
Arlington, VA 22203-5190
(703) 696-5806
(703) 696-6344 FAX

National Adoption Center
1500 Walnut Street, Suite 701
Philadelphia, PA 19102
(800) 862-3678
(215) 735-9410 FAX

National Alliance for the Mentally
Ill
200 N. Glebe Rd., Suite 1015
Arlington, VA 22203-3754
(800) 950-6264
(703) 524-9094 FAX

National Association of Anorexia
Nervosa & Associated Disorders
(ANAD)
Box 7
Highland Park, IL 60035
(708) 831-3438
(708) 433-4632 FAX

National Association for Childcare
Resource & Referral Agencies
2116 Campus Drive, S.E.
Rochester, MN 55904
(800) 462-1660
(507) 287-2411 FAX

National Association for the
Education of Young Children
1509 16th Street, N.W.
Washington, D.C. 20036-1426
(800) 424-2460
(202) 328-1846 FAX

National Association of Former
Foster Children, Inc.
P.O. Box 874
New York, NY 10268-0874
(212) 332-0078

National Association of Homes and
Services for Children
1701 K. Street, N.W., Suite 200
Washington, D.C. 20006-1503
(800) 220-1016
(202) 331-7476 FAX

National Association of Services
and Conservation Corps
666 11th Street, N.W., Suite 500
Washington, D.C. 20001
(202) 737-6272
(202) 737-6277

National Black Child Development
Institute, Inc.
1023 15th Street, N.W., Suite 600
Washington, D.C. 20005
(800) 556-2234
(202) 234-1738 FAX

National Center on Child Abuse
and Neglect
P.O. Box 1182
Washington, D.C. 20013
(800) 394-3366
(202) 205-8221 FAX

National Center on Institutions &
Alternatives
635 Slaters Lane, Suite G-100
Alexandria, VA 22314
(703) 684-0373
(703) 549-4077 FAX

National Center for Missing and
Exploited Children
2101 Wilson Blvd., Suite 550
Arlington, VA 22201
(703) 235-3900
(800) 843-5678 Report Information
Line
(703) 235-4067 FAX

National Center for Youth Law
114 Sansome Street, Suite 900
San Francisco, CA 94104
(415) 543-3307
(415) 956-9024 FAX

National Child Labor Committee
1501 Broadway, Room 1111
New York, NY 10036
(212) 840-1801
(212) 768-0963 FAX

National Child Safety Council
P.O. Box 1368
Jackson, MI 49204
(517) 764-6070
(517) 764-3068 FAX

National Coalition Against
Domestic Violence
P.O. Box 18749
Denver, CO 80218-0749
(303) 839-1852
(303) 831-9251 FAX

National Coalition for Hispanic
Health & Human Services
(COSSMHO)
1501 16th Street
Washington, D.C. 20036
(202) 387-5000
(202) 797-4353 FAX

National Committee to Prevent
Child Abuse (NCPCA)
332 South Michigan Ave., Suite 1600
Chicago, IL 60604
(800) 244-5373
(312) 939-8962 FAX

National Council for Adoption
1930 17th Street, N.W.
Washington, D.C. 20009
(202) 328-1200
(202) 332-0935 FAX

National Council on Child Abuse
and Family Violence
1155 Connecticut Ave., N.W.,
Suite 400
Washington, D.C. 20036
(800) 222-2000
(202) 467-4924 FAX

National Council on Crime &
Delinquency
685 Market Street, Suite 620
San Francisco, CA 94105
(415) 896-6223
(415) 896-5109 FAX

National Council on Family
Relations
3989 Central Ave., N.E., Suite 550
Columbia Heights, MN 55421
(612) 781-9331
(612) 781-9348 FAX

National Council of Jewish Women
53 West 23rd Street
New York, NY 10010
(212) 645-4048
(212) 645-7466 FAX

National Council of Negro Women
1001 G Street, N.W., Suite 800
Washington, D.C. 20001
(202) 628-0015
(202) 628-0233 FAX

National Court Appointed Special
Advocate Association (CASA)
2722 Eastlake Ave., East, Suite 220
Seattle, WA 98102
(800) 628-3233
(206) 323-8137 FAX

National Crime Prevention Council
1700 K Street, N.W., 2nd Floor
Washington, D.C. 20006-3817
(202) 466-6272
(202) 296-1356 FAX

National Criminal Justice Reference
Service (NCJRS)
1600 Research Boulevard
Rockville, MD 20850
(800) 851-3420

Justice Statistics Clearinghouse
(800) 732-3277

National Victims Resource Center
(800) 627-6872

Justice Assistance Clearinghouse
(800) 688-4252

National Diabetes Information
Clearinghouse
Box NDIC—One Information Way
Bethesda, MD 20892-3560
(301) 654-3327
(301) 907-8906 FAX

The National Directory of Children,
Youth & Families Services
P.O. Box 1837
Longmont, CO 80502-1837
(800) 343-6681
(303) 776-5831 FAX

National Down Syndrome Society
666 Broadway, Suite 800
New York, NY 10012-2317
(800) 221-4602
(212) 979-2873 FAX

National Easter Seal Society
230 W. Monroe St., Suite 1800
Chicago, IL 60606
(800) 221-6827
(312) 726-4258 TDD

National Education Association
1201 16th Street, N.W.
Washington, D.C. 20036
(202) 833-4000
(202) 822-7974 FAX

National Exchange Club
Foundation for the Prevention of
Child Abuse
3050 Central Ave.
Toledo, OH 43606
(419) 535-3232
(419) 535-1989 FAX

National Fathers' Network
16120 N.E. Eighth Street
Bellevue, WA 98008
(206) 747-4004 or (206) 284-2859

National Foster Parent Association
226 Kilts Drive
Houston, TX 77024-6214
(713) 467-1850
(713) 827-0919 FAX

National 4-H Council
7100 Connecticut Ave.
Chevy Chase, MD 20815
(301) 961-2800
(301) 961-2894 FAX

National Head Start Association
201 N. Union St., Suite 320
Alexandria, VA 22314
(703) 739-0875
(703) 739-0878 FAX

National Health Information Center
P.O. Box 1133
Washington, D.C. 20013-1133
(800) 336-4797
(301) 468-7394 FAX

National Hospital for Kids in Crisis
5300 KidsPeace Drive
Orefield, PA 18069
(800) 446-9543
(215) 799-8801 FAX

National Information Center for
Children & Youth with Disabilities
P.O. Box 1492
Washington, D.C. 20013
(800) 695-0285
(202) 884-8441 FAX

National Information Center for
Deafness (NICD)
800 Florida Ave., N.E.
Washington, D.C. 20002
(202) 651-5051
(202) 651-5052 TDD
(202) 651-5054 FAX

National Institute for Citizen
Education in Law
711 G St., S.E.
Washington, D.C. 20003
(202) 546-6644
(202) 546-6649 FAX

National Job Corps Alumni
Association
607 14th St., N.W., Suite 610
Washington, D.C. 20005
(800) 424-2866
(800) 733-5627 HOTLINE
(202) 638-3807 FAX

National Kidney & Urologic
Diseases Information Clearinghouse
3 Information Way
Bethesda, MD 20892-3580
(301) 654-4415

National Lekotek Center
2100 Ridge Ave.
Evanston, IL 60201-2796
(800) 366-7529
(708) 328-5514 FAX

National Organization for Victim
Assistance
1757 Park Rd., N.W.
Washington, D.C. 20010
(800) 879-6682
(202) 462-2255 FAX

National PTA Headquarters
330 N. Wabash Ave., Suite 2100
Chicago, IL 60611-2511
(312) 670-6782
(312) 670-6783 FAX

National Pediatric HIV Resource
Center
15 South Ninth Street
Newark, NJ 07107
(800) 362-0071
(201) 485-2752 FAX

National Rehabilitation Information
Center
8455 Colesville Rd., Suite 935
Silver Springs, MD 20910-3319
(800) 346-2742 TDD & Voice
(301) 587-1967 FAX

National Resource Center for
Family Centered Practice
112 North Hall
Iowa City, IA 52242
(319) 335-2200
(319) 335-2204 FAX

National School Boards Association
1680 Duke Street
Alexandria, VA 22314
(703) 838-6722

National Urban League
500 East 62nd Street
New York, NY 10021
(212) 310-9000
(212) 593-8250 FAX

National Victim Center
309 West 7th St., Suite 705
Ft. Worth, TX 76102
(800) 394-2255
(817) 877-3396 FAX

National Youth Employment
Coalition
1001 Connecticut Ave., N.W.,
Suite 719
Washington, D.C. 20036
(202) 659-1064
(202) 775-9733 FAX

Obsessive Compulsive Disorder
Foundation
P.O. Box 70
Milford, CT 06460
(203) 878-5669

Orphan Foundation of America
1500 Massachusetts Ave., N.W.,
Suite 448
Washington, D.C. 20005
(800) 950-4673
(202) 223-9079 FAX

Pacific Institute for Research &
Evaluation
7315 Wisconsin Ave., Suite 1300
West
Bethesda, MD 20814
(301) 951-4233
(301) 907-8637 FAX

Parents Helping Parents, Inc.
3041 Olcott Street
Santa Clara, CA 95054
(408) 727-5775

Pretrial Services Resource Center
1325 G St., N.W., Suite 1020
Washington, D.C. 20005
(202) 638-3080
(202) 347-0493 FAX

Resources for Children with Special
Needs, Inc.
200 Park Ave., South, Suite 816
New York, NY 10003
(212) 677-4650
(212) 254-4070 FAX

The Salvation Army National
Headquarters
P.O. Box 269
615 Slaters Lane
Alexandria, VA 22313-0269
(703) 684-5500
(703) 684-3478 FAX

Save the Children International &
National Office
54 Wilton Road
Westport, CT 06880
(203) 221-4000
(203) 454-3914 FAX

Survivors of Incest Anonymous,
Inc.
World Service Office
P.O. Box 21817
Baltimore, MD 21222
(410) 282-3400

ToughLove International
P.O. Box 1069
100 Mechanic Street
Doylestown, PA 18901
(800) 333-1069
(215) 348-9874 FAX

United Cerebral Palsy Association
1160 L St., N.W., Suite 700
Washington, D.C. 20036

United Jewish Appeal-Federation of
Jewish Philanthropies of NY
130 East 59th Street
New York, NY 10022
(212) 980-1000
(212) 888-7538 FAX

U.S. Catholic Conference
3211 4th Street, N.E.
Washington, D.C. 20017-1194
(202) 541-3000
(202) 541-3322 FAX

U.S. Center for Disease Control &
Prevention National AIDS
Clearinghouse
P.O. Box 6003
Rockville, MD 20849-6003
(800) 458-5231
(800) 243-7012 Deaf Access Line
(TTY/TDD)
(301) 217-0023 International Line
(301) 738-6616 FAX

Volunteers of America National
Headquarters Office
3939 North Causeway Blvd., Suite
400
Metairie, LA 70002-1784
(800) 899-0089
(504) 837-4200 FAX

Women in Community Service
(WICS)
1900 N. Beauregard St., Suite 103
Alexandria, VA 22311
(800) 442-9427
(703) 671-4489 FAX

World Association for Infant Mental
Health
Kellogg Building #27
Michigan State University
E. Lansing, MI 48824-1022
(517) 432-3793

YWCA of The U.S.A. National
Board
726 Broadway
New York, NY 10003
(212) 614-2700
(212) 677-9716 FAX

Youth Policy Institute
1221 Massachusetts Ave., N.W.,
Suite B
Washington, D.C. 20005
(202) 638-2144
(202) 638-2325 FAX

Youth Service America
1101 15th St., N.W., Suite 200
Washington, D.C 20005
(202) 296-2992
(202) 296-4030 FAX

Canadian Federal Agencies

Canada provides health care programs to its citizens through the Department of National Health in conjunction with the provinces and municipalities. The Department of Human Resources Development provides income maintenance and social service programs. Programs are supported by a combination of federal-provincial-municipal funding.

Related federal agencies have responsibility for Indian affairs and development of the territories, work force resources, employment services, immigration, unemployment compensation, and veterans affairs.

Department of National Health

The department is composed of five branches. The program branches are described in the following paragraphs.

Policy and Consultation Branch

The objective of the Policy and Consultation Branch is to provide advice to the Minister, Deputy Minister, and program branches on social and health trends and issues, policy requirements, strategic planning, and information needs relative to departmental objectives, priorities, and programs. The branch undertakes policy research and analysis and coordinates many major policy initiatives within the department.

The Communications Directorate provides strategic communications advice, media and public relations, and publishing and distribution services and organizes conferences and special events.

The newly created Women's Health Bureau plays an advocacy, liaison, and education role with other government and nongovernmental organizations to ensure that Canada's health care system responds to issues affecting women's health.

The branch is also responsible not only for Canada's participation in matters involving international and federal/provincial liaison in the areas of health and social affairs, but also for developing Canada's position on international health issues, advising on bilateral relations with foreign governments, and monitoring international health matters. Finally, the branch administers the Access to Information Act and the Privacy Act, coordinates Canada's drug strategy, and coordinates, monitors, and advises on departmental policies and programs as they relate to women and their families.

Health Protection Branch

This branch is concerned with protecting the health of Canadians. Its role is "to protect and improve the well-being of the Canadian public by defining, advising on, and managing risks to health."

The branch identifies, assesses, and manages risks to health associated with food, drugs (including immunizing agents and biologics), radiation-emitting and medical devices, consumer products, and environmental contaminants. It also investigates the occurrence and cause of communicable and noncommunicable diseases, and injury. These activities require extensive cooperation with provincial health agencies and authorities, with provincially authorized professional licensing bodies, service institutions, universities, and international agencies.

The responsibility for protecting Canadians from certain types of health hazards, such as environmental contaminants, is shared with other federal departments, and often entails interagency cooperation across the two levels of government.

The branch supports health care services provided by the provinces by ensuring the safety and effectiveness of the drugs and devices on which medicine depends, and by providing national laboratory facilities for diagnostic reference services and the evaluation of diagnostic reagents and methods. The branch also provides specialized analytical services and expert testimony for national, provincial, and local law enforcement agencies that control drug abuse and trafficking.

Medical Services Branch

The branch provides health services, health promotion, and assessment services to a wide clientele through the following programs:

Indian and Northern Health Services. Assists status Indians, Inuit, and residents of the Yukon Territory to attain a level of health comparable to that of other Canadians.

Noninsured Health Benefits. Provides health benefits to Inuit and status Indians beyond those paid by provincial governments.

Program Transfer, Policy, and Planning. Works with native communities to help them take control over the administration and the delivery of health care within their own communities.

Occupational and Environmental Health. Provides an occupational health and safety program for the Public Service and provides environmental health services to native communities.

Health Advisory Services. Provides medical assessments of immigrants and civil aviation personnel. In addition it ensures the provision of health and social services under national emergency conditions.

Health Programs and Services Branch

The primary responsibility of this branch is to develop, promote, and support measures designed to preserve and improve the health and social well-being of Canadian residents. The branch also has a major role in providing leadership and coordination in assisting the provinces and territories to bring their health services to, and maintain them at, national standards.

Children's Bureau

The main role of the Children's Bureau is to encourage effective policies and programs relating to the health, welfare, and development of children and families. The bureau promotes coordination within the federal government and consults with other levels of government and nongovernmental organizations on federal initiatives relating to children. The bureau is responsible for the coordination of Canada's implementation of the United Nations Convention on the Rights of the Child, ratified on December 11, 1991, and is currently preparing Canada's progress report to the United Nations.

In addition, the bureau has developed Canada's Action Plan for Children, which is Canada's response to the World Summit for Children. It provides a framework for addressing the long-term needs of Canadian children and has served as a basis for the development of Brighter Futures, a comprehensive five-year federal strategy announced in May 1992, to improve the lives of Canadian children.

The bureau is also responsible for the implementation and coordination of the Brighter Futures initiative, a group of long-term programs designed to address conditions of risk during the earliest years in a child's life.

In addition, Canada has a long-standing commitment to working with other countries to address global issues, and Canada has worked for the welfare of the world's children by participating with multilateral organizations and by maintaining bilateral relations.

The Partners for Children Fund, administered by the Children's Bureau, represents the federal government's response to the Declaration on the Survival, Protection, and Development of Children and the Plan of Action. The purpose of the fund is to support projects that demonstrate Canada's continuing commitment to action as a result of the World Summit recommendations through appropriate nongovernmental and nonprofit organizations working internationally to improve the lives of children.

Seniors Secretariat

A Seniors Secretariat provides information and support to the Minister of State for Seniors. This secretariat is responsible for the following functions: (1) meeting with federal government departments and agencies to coordinate and encourage programs and policies for seniors; (2) consulting with provincial governments on matters related to seniors; (3) consulting with organizations for seniors, professional groups, voluntary associations, and individual seniors to learn more about seniors' needs; (4) developing a communications program to inform seniors of the services and benefits available to them and to keep decision makers aware of the real needs of Canada's seniors; and providing, at the federal level, an information and referral service. Seniors community programs such as New Horizons, Seniors Independence programs, and Ventures in Independence are contribution programs for older Canadians. Seniors and other stakeholders can work together on issues that promote the independence and quality of life of Canada's aging population.

New Horizons

The New Horizons Program encourages older, retired Canadians to share their skills, talents, and experience through activities that are of benefit to themselves and to their community. The program provides financial help to assist seniors to join with others of their age in group projects that they themselves initiate, organize, develop, and control.

Seniors Independence Program

This program provides financial assistance to eligible groups for health, education, and social well-being projects designed to enhance the quality of life and independence of seniors. Seniors must be actively involved in project design and delivery. Priority is given to community-based projects that direct attention to the needs of women seniors, seniors living in rural and remote areas, and seniors who are less advantaged due to life circumstances.

Ventures in Independence

This program offers business, labor, and other levels of government increased coinvestment opportunities with seniors.

Family Violence Prevention Division

Established in December 1986 to coordinate federal involvement and leadership in the area of family violence, the division, in consultation with the provinces, territories, professional associations, and nongovernmental organizations, promotes the development and implementation of policies, programs, and community-based services relating to the prevention and reduction of family violence. It has been responsible for coordinating funding mechanisms and processes within the federal government under the Family Violence and Child Sexual Abuse Initiatives. A new four-year (1991–1995) federal Family Violence Initiative ensures continuity of funding to increase public awareness of the problem, encourage effective prevention efforts, improve the skills and knowledge of workers, enhance information exchange, and improve treatment and support for victims, their families, and offenders.

The division includes the National Clearinghouse on Family Violence, which provides resource materials and a referral service to professionals and the public on all aspects of family violence.

Human Resources Development Canada

Income Security Programs Branch

This branch is responsible for the administration of the Canada Pension Plan, the Old Age Security Program, and the Children's Special Allowances program.

Canada Pension Plan

The Canada Pension Plan is a contributory social insurance program designed to provide a basic level of income protection against the contingencies of retirement, disability, and death. The plan operates in all parts of Canada, except in the province of Québec where a similar program, the Québec Pension Plan (QPP) is in force. The plan provides three main types of benefits: retirement pensions, disability pensions for contributors and benefits for their dependent children, and survivors benefits consisting of a lump-sum death benefit payable to the deceased contributor's estate, a monthly pension for the surviving spouse, and monthly benefits for dependent children.

Old Age Security

Under the Old Age Security (OAS) Act, pensions are paid on a universal, noncontributory basis to those aged sixty-five and over who meet certain residence requirements. A Guaranteed Income Supplement (GIS) may be added to the basic pension in the case of pensioners who have little or no income outside of their basic OAS pension. Likewise, a Spouse's Allowance (SPA) may be paid on an income-tested basis to the spouse of an OAS/GIS pensioner if the spouse is sixty to sixty-four years of age and meets the residence requirements. A similar benefit is available to sixty to sixty-four-year-old widow(er)s.

Children's Special Allowances

The Children's Special Allowances are amounts paid to assist in the support of children under the care of provincial departments, agencies, and institutions, including children in foster care. The monthly amount is equivalent to the basic amount of the Child Tax Benefit.

Social Service Programs Branch

This branch administers three major federal-provincial cost-sharing programs and five grants and contributions programs. It has responsibility for developing and implementing the federal approach on child care, family violence, and seniors. It also has responsibility for coordinating departmental activities related to the National Strategy for the Integration of Persons with Disabilities. It provides consultation and advice to provincial officials, voluntary organizations, and consumer groups on family and children's services, community development, voluntary actions, and rehabilitation. The Seniors Secretariat supports the Minister of State for Seniors by enhancing the quality of life for Canada's seniors.

Cost-Shared Programs Directorate

This directorate administers all department programs that are based on cost-sharing agreements with the provinces.

Canada Assistance Plan

Under agreements signed with all provinces and territories, the federal government, through the Canada Assistance Plan (CAP), shares eligible costs that these jurisdictions and their municipalities incur in the provision of a wide range of social assistance and welfare service programs to needy persons.

CAP shares in the cost of the following programs that are administered by the province.

Financial Assistance—Provinces and territories receive cost sharing for assistance they and their municipalities provide to persons in need. Assistance must be provided on the basis of a test of need which takes into account an individual's budgetary requirements and any income and resources available to meet these requirements. Assistance includes aid to persons in need for basic requirements (i.e., food, shelter, clothing, fuel, utilities, household supplies, and personal requirements) and may also include aid for travel and transportation, for certain health services (such as drugs and dental care) and for special needs as determined by each province or territory such as civil legal aid, wheelchairs, prostheses, and essential repairs to homes.

Institutional Care—Federal sharing is available to the provinces and territories of costs they and their municipalities incur in the provision of residential care to persons in need of facilities that qualify as homes for special care under CAP (i.e., homes for the aged, nursing homes, child-care facilities, hostels for transients, and shelters for battered women).

Since April 1, 1977, cost sharing of residential care for adult persons in need has been limited under CAP due to the introduction of new funding arrangements pursuant to the Extended Health Care Services Program of the Federal-Provincial Fiscal Arrangements and Federal Post-Secondary Education and Health Contributions Act, which subsumed the major responsibility for federal financial support to the provinces and territories for long-term adult residential care.

Certain facilities providing short-term residential care to adults are not included in this new financing arrangement and, consequently, CAP continues to share in the full cost to the provinces and territories of maintaining adult persons in need in these facilities (i.e., hostels for transients, homes for unmarried mothers, and crisis intervention centers such as shelters for battered women).

There has been no change to the capacity of CAP to share in the cost to the provinces and territories of providing residential care to children who qualify as persons in need within the scope of the plan. Cost sharing in residential care for children under CAP was not affected by the funding arrangement pursuant to the Federal-Provincial Fiscal Arrangements and Federal Post-Secondary Education and Health Contributions Act.

Welfare Services—The federal government shares in certain costs to the provinces and territories that they and their municipalities incur in providing welfare services to persons in need and persons likely to become in need. Welfare services are defined as services having as their objective the lessening, removal, or prevention of the causes and effects of poverty, child neglect, or dependence on public assistance and include day-care services, homemaker services, counseling services, adoption services, rehabilitation services, information and referral services on a wide range of child welfare services, as well as the administration of public assistance programs.

Work Activity Projects—Under CAP the federal government shares in costs that provinces and territories incur in operating work activity projects. These projects provide a comprehensive approach to social rehabilitation in that they are aimed at resolving the personal, family, or environmental problems of persons who have difficulty in securing or maintaining employment or in undertaking training. Projects are designed to help improve the motivation and work capacity of participants and prepare them for entry or return to employment or further vocational training.

Vocational Rehabilitation of Disabled Persons

Under agreements signed with all the provinces and territories, the federal government, through the Vocational Rehabilitation of Disabled Persons Act (VRDP), contributes 50 percent of the costs incurred by the provinces toward a comprehensive vocational rehabilitation program for physically and mentally disabled persons. As of April 1, 1990, a new three-year agreement with all provinces and territories took effect.

Services to individuals under a comprehensive vocational rehabilitation program include assessment; counseling; restorative services; provision of prostheses, wheelchairs, technical aids, and other devices; vocational training and employment placement; provision of tools, books, and equipment necessary for employment; maintenance allowances as required by each individual; follow-up goods and services; and goods and services to prevent the loss of employment of disabled persons facing a vocational crisis. Recent initiatives include establishing appeal procedures for disabled persons who are refused service because they are deemed ineligible.

There is also provision within the VRDP to fund vocational rehabilitation research projects undertaken by individual researchers and organizations. This fund is administered by the National Welfare Grants Division of the Social Services Program Branch.

Alcohol and Drug Treatment and Rehabilitation

This new federal-provincial cost-sharing agreement, which took effect April 1, 1988, is a component of Canada's Drug Strategy announced in 1987. It enables the federal government to extend financial support to provinces in order to increase the availability of alcohol and drug programming in Canada. Youths are the prime target group; however, other groups at risk, such as women and the elderly, are also being served. This agreement complements the VRDP, which supports provincial programming for alcohol and drug treatment and rehabilitation in the context of vocational rehabilitation. The initial two-year agreement, developed jointly with the provinces, has been signed by eight provinces. A new three-year agreement took effect as of April 1, 1990. Negotiations continue with the remaining provinces and territories to conclude the new (1990–1993) agreement. Services covered in the agreement include assessment, early intervention, special access services, detoxification, counseling, aftercare, information on the availability and accessibility of services, and work initiatives.

Social Development Directorate

This directorate provides contributions to community groups, social service organizations, schools of social work, individuals, and other levels of government for research and demonstration activities. It also provides sustaining grants to national voluntary social service organizations. The directorate is responsible for the National Welfare Grants, National Adoption Desk, Disabled Persons Unit, Family Violence Prevention Division, child-care programs, New Horizons program, and the Seniors Independence program.

National Welfare Grants

This is a national and social research and development program that provides consultation and financial support to stimulate knowledge development, identify social policy and service needs and gaps, and recommend action in critical areas of social welfare.

National Adoption Desk

The National Adoption Desk represents provincial and territorial (except Québec) adoption authorities in dealings with foreign authorities on intercountry adoption matters, provides consultative and liaison services to the provinces/territories in the area of international adoption, negotiates intercountry adoption agreements and programs, and coordinates adoption cases between provincial/territorial and foreign authorities.

Child-Care Programs Division

This division has three principal components: the Child Care Initiatives Fund (CCIF), the Child Care Regional Consultants, and the National Child Care Information Centre (NCCIC). The CCIF, announced in 1987, supports research, development, and demonstration projects relating to child care over a seven-year period. The Child Care Regional Consultants are liaison officers between the provincial/territorial government and the federal government who provide advice and consultation to groups and organizations regarding child-care issues as well as the CCIF. The NCCIC is a national focal point for information and promotion of quality child-care services in Canada. Current literature is available, free of charge, on a wide range of child-care matters. The NCCIC has a resource center with a diverse selection of information and research data on child-care issues, and a distribution center that disseminates publications, articles, fact sheets, posters, and information kits on relevant child-care issues.

Disabled Persons Unit

The mandate of this unit is to promote and support the development of programs and initiatives that enhance opportunities for disabled persons to live and work within the community. Working extensively with nongovernment and private sector groups and individuals, the unit provides a consultation and brokerage function whereby resources of government and nongovernment sectors are effectively linked to initiatives of merit in the area of services to disabled persons.

Under the National Strategy for the Integration of Persons with Disabilities, the Disabled Persons Unit also administers the Ability Program, which provides funding in support of initiatives that advance the community and economic integration of persons with disabilities and social integration of children and youths with disabilities.

Where to Write

Inquiries regarding **federal health programs** should be addressed to:
Communications Branch
Department of National Health
Jeanne Mance Bldg., 19th Fl.
Ottawa, ON K1A 0K9

Inquiries regarding **federal income security and social service programs** should be addressed to:
Communications Branch
Human Resources Development Canada
140 Promenade du Portage
Hull, PQ K1A 0J9

Inquiries regarding **welfare, social services, and health care programs administered by the provinces and territories** should be addressed to the appropriate provincial or territorial agency (see the **Where to Write** sections for each province and territory).

Department of National Health

Office of the Minister
Jeanne Mance Bldg.
Ottawa, ON K1A 0K9
Tel: (613) 957-0200
Diane Marleau, M.P., Min.,
(613) 957-0200

Office of the Deputy Minister
Michele S. Jean, Dep. Min.,
(613) 957-0213
Susan Fletcher, Exec. Dir., National
Advisory Council on Aging,
(613) 957-1971

Corporate Services Branch
Robert Lafleur, Asst. Dep. Min.,
(613) 952-3984
O. Marquardt, Dir. Gen., Financial
Administration, (613) 957-7762
J. Butler, Dir., Departmental
Administration, (613) 952-0947
M. Williams, Dir. Gen., Facilities
Mgmt. Srvs., (613) 957-3375
H. Valin, Act. Dir., Departmental
Srvs., (613) 957-9247
B. Smith, Dir., Parliamentary
Relations, (613) 952-0665
S. Harisson, Dir., CMB, Exec.
Secretariat, (613) 952-4104
F. Bull, Dir. Gen., Informatics,
(613) 954-8713

Human Resources Directorate
Robert Joubert, Dir. Gen.,
(613) 957-3236

Communications Directorate
Joel Weiner, Dir. Gen.,
(613) 957-2979
Sandra Lavigne, Dir., Operations
and Planning Div., (613) 957-2981
Carole Peacock, Dir., Media and
Pub. Relations Div., (613) 957-2987;
FAX: (613) 952-7266

Policy and Consultation Branch
André Juneau, Asst. Dep. Min.,
(613) 957-3059

Judith Ferguson, Dir. Gen., Health
Policy, (613) 957-3066
Health Policy Division
Guy Bujold, Dir., (613) 957-3081
Strategic Planning Division
Lyle Makosky, Dir., (613) 957-3026
Canada Drug Strategy Secretariat
I. Malyalewsky, Exec. Dir.,
(613) 957-3507
Women's Health Bureau
Abby Hoffman, Dir., (613) 957-1940

International Affairs Directorate
E.M. Aiston, Act. Dir. Gen.
Health Affairs Directorate
E.M. Aiston, Dir., (613) 957-7298
International Information and
Planning Directorate
Patricia Dunn Erickson, Chf.,
(613) 957-7288
Social Development Directorate
D. Ogston, Dir. Gen., (613) 957-8672

Medical Services Branch
Jeanne Mance Bldg.
de l'Eglantine St.
Ottawa, ON K1A 0L3
Marie Fortier, Act. Asst. Dep. Min.,
(613) 957-7701
Public Service Health
G.I. Lynch, Dir. Gen., (613) 957-7669
Indian and Northern Health
Services
M. McNaughton, Dir. Gen.,
(613) 952-9616
Health Advisory Services
L. Davies, Act. Dir. Gen.,
(613) 957-7665
Program Transfer and Policy
Planning
P. Blais, Act. Dir. Gen.,
(613) 957-3402

Health Protection Branch
Kent Foster, Asst. Dep. Min.,
(613) 957-1804
Drugs Directorate
D. Michols, Dir. Gen., (613) 957-0369

Food Directorate
S.W. Gunner, Dir. Gen.,
(613) 957-1821
Field Operations
J.R. Elliott, Dir., (613) 957-1794
Environmental Health Directorate
R. Hickman, Dir. Gen.,
(613) 954-0291
Laboratory Centre for Disease
Control
J. Losos, Dir. Gen., (613) 957-0315
Finance and Administration
Directorate
M.T. McElrone, Dir., (613) 957-1014

**Health Programs and Services
Branch**
Jeanne Mance Bldg.
de l'Eglantine St.
Ottawa, ON K1A 1B4
Kay Stanley, Asst. Dep. Min.,
(613) 954-8524
Health Insurance
Bruce Davis, Dir. Gen.,
(613) 954-8674
Health Services
Diane Kirkpatrick, Dir. Gen.,
(613) 954-8629
Extramural Research Programs
Mary Ellen Jeans, Dir. Gen.,
(613) 954-8538
Health Promotion
Catherine Lane, Dir. Gen.,
(613) 957-7792
Policy and Planning
Judy Lockette, Dir., (613) 954-8532
Office of the Principal Nursing
Officer
M.J. Flaherty, (613) 957-1975
Seniors Secretariat
S. Hansen, Exec. Dir., (613) 954-8536
New Horizons Program
E. Kwavnick, Dir., (613) 957-2881
Family Violence Programs
E. Scott, Dir., (613) 957-0622
Seniors Independence Program
D. O'Flaherty, Dir., (613) 952-9529

Human Resources Development Canada

140 Promenade du Portage
Hull, PQ K1A 0J9
Lloyd Axworthy, Min.,
(819) 994-2482

Jean-Jacques Noreau, Dep. Min.,
(819) 994-4514
François Pouliot, Assoc. Dep. Min.,
(819) 994-4520

Strategic Policy
Harvey Lazar, Sr. Asst. Dep. Min.,
(819) 994-4272
Kathy O'Hara, Asst. Dep. Min.,
(819) 997-1094

Employment
Kristina Liljefors, Exec. Dir.,
(819) 953-7362

Human Resource Services
Jean Claude Bouchard, Asst. Dep.
Min., (613) 994-1791

Insurance
Hy Braiter, Exec. Dir.,
(819) 994-1600

Systems
David McNaughton, Exec. Mgr.,
(819) 994-1592

Financial and Administrative
Services
W.E.R. (Bob) Little, Asst. Dep. Min.,
(819) 994-2521

Income Security Programs
Monique Plante, Asst. Dep. Min.,
(819) 957-3111

Labour
Michael McDermott, Sr. Asst. Dep.
Min., (819) 997-1493

Social Development and Education
Ian C. Green, Asst. Dep. Min.,
(819) 957-2953

Related Federal Agencies

**Department of Indian Affairs and
Northern Development**
Les Terrasses de la Chaudière
10 Wellington St., North Tower
Hull, PQ K1A 0H4
Tel: (819) 997-0002
Ronald A. Irwin, Min.,
(819) 997-0002
Dan Goodleaf, Dep. Min.,
(819) 997-0133
Richard Van Loon, Assoc. Dep.
Min., (819) 997-0854
Claims and Indian Government
John Sinclair, Asst. Dep. Min.,
(819) 953-3180
Policy and Strategic Direction
Jack Stagg, Asst. Dep. Min.,
(819) 994-7555
Lands and Trust Services
Wendy F. Porteous, Asst. Dep. Min.,
(819) 953-5577
Northern Affairs
John Rayner, Asst. Dep. Min.,
(819) 953-3760
Corporate Services
Alan Williams, Asst. Dep. Min.,
(819) 997-0020
Regional Directors General
Gerry Kerr, Atlantic, (902) 661-6262

Guy McKenzie, Québec,
(418) 648-3270
Audrey Doerr, Ontario,
(416) 973-6201
Brenda D. Kustra, Manitoba,
(204) 983-2475
Myler Savill, Saskatchewan,
(306) 780-5950
Ken Kirby, Alberta, (403) 495-2835
John Watson, British Columbia,
(604) 666-5201
Mike Ivanski, Yukon, (403) 667-3300
Warren Johnson, Northwest
Territories, (403) 920-8111

Ministry of the Solicitor General
Sir Wilfrid Laurier Bldg.
340 Laurier Ave., West
Ottawa, ON K1A 0P8
Tel: (613) 995-7548
Herb Gray, Sol. Gen., (613) 991-2924
Correctional Service of Canada
John Edwards, Comm.,
 (613) 995-5481
National Parole Board
Michel Dagenais, Chair,
(613) 954-1150
Royal Canadian Mounted Police
N.D. Inkster, Comm., (613) 993-0400

Canadian Security Intelligence
Service
Raymond Protti, Dir., (613) 993-9620

Department of Veteran Affairs
Daniel J. MacDonald Bldg.
P.O. Box 7700
Charlottetown, PE C1A 8M9
Tel: (902) 566-8330
66 Slater St.
Ottawa, ON K1A 0P4
David Collenette, Min., National
Defence and Veterans Affairs,
(613) 996-3100
David Nicholson, Dep. Min.,
(613) 996-6881
Veterans Services
(Vacant), Asst. Dep. Min.,
(902) 566-8100
Administration
S. Rainville, Asst. Dep. Min.,
(902) 566-8047
Veterans Appeal Board
T. Whalen, Chair, (902) 566-8636
Canadian Pension Commission
M. Chartier, Chair, (902) 566-8800
Bureau of Pensions Advocates
Keith Bell, Chf. Pensions Advocate,
(902) 566-8640

Department of Health Canada

Office of the Minister
Brooke Claxton Building
Ottawa, ON K1A 0K9
Tel: (613) 957-0200
The Honorable Allan Rock
(613) 957-0200

Office of the Deputy Minister
Michèle S. Jean, Deputy Minister
(613) 957-0213
Alan Nymark, Associate Deputy
Minister (613) 954-5904
Sylvie Dufresne, Director General,
Departmental Secretariat
(613) 941-2000
Hélène Valin, Director,
Departmental Service (613) 957-9247
Bob Houston, Director,
Parliamentary Relations
(613) 952-0665

Corporate Services Branch
Robert S. Lafleur, Senior Associate
Deputy Minister (613) 952-3984
Gordon Peters, Director, Internal
Audit (613) 957-4362
Orvel Marquardt, Director General,
Departmental Planning and
Financial Administration
Directorate (613) 957-7762
Robert Joubert, Director General,
Human Resources Directorate
(613) 957-3236
Marie Williams, Director General,
Assets Management Directorate
(613) 957-3375
Fruji Bull, Director General,
Information Management Services
Directorate (613) 954-8713

Policy and Consultation Branch
André Juneau, Assistant Deputy
Minister (613) 957-3059
Abby Hoffman, Director General,
Women's Health Bureau
(613) 957-1940
Malcolm Brown, Director General,
Intergovernmental Affairs
Directorate (613) 957-3081
Sange de Silva, Director General,
Strategic Planning and Review

Directorate (613) 954-8072
Director General, Health Policy and
Information Directorate
(613) 957-3066
Ed Aiston, Director General,
International Affairs Directorate
(613) 957-7298
Patricia Dunn Erickson, Director,
International Information Division
(613) 957-7288
Andrew Simon, Director General,
Office of Health and the
Information Highway
(613) 954-7532
Carla Gilders, Director General,
Communications and Consultation
Directorate (613) 957-2979
Director, Communications Services
(613) 957-2987

Health Promotion and Programs Branch
Jeanne Mance Building
Ottawa, On K1A 0K9
Ian Potter, Assistant Deputy
Minister (613) 954-8525
Judy Lockett, A/Director General,
Management Planning and
Operations Directorate
(613) 954-8532
Catherine Lane, Director General,
Population Health Directorate
(613) 957-7792
Nancy Garrard, Director, Division
of Aging and Seniors (613) 957-1967
Jim Mintz, Director, Partnerships
and Marketing Division
(613) 954-2402
Diane C. Kirkpatrick, Director
General, Strategies and Systems for
Health Directorate (613) 954-8629
Janet Davies, Director, Health Issues
(613) 941-1977
David Allan, Family Violence
(613) 957-2866

Health Protection Branch
Health Protection Building
Ottawa, On K1A 0K9
Dr. Joseph Z. Losos, Assistant
Deputy Minister (613) 957-1804

Ian Shugart, Visiting Assistant
Deputy Minister (613) 941-4332
Joel Weiner, Executive Director,
Office of Scientific and Regulatory
Affairs (613) 952-3665
Executive Director, Office of
Laboratory Rationalization
(613) 957-7894
Dann M. Michols, Director General,
Therapeutic Products Directorate
(613) 957-0369
Dr. George Paterson, Director
General, Food Directorate
(613) 957-1821
Rod Raphael, A/Director General,
Environmental Health Directorate
(613) 954-0291
Dr. Michael Shannon, Director
General, Laboratory Centre for
Disease Control (613) 957-0316
Radiation Protection Bureau
(613) 954-6647

Medical Services Branch
Jeanne Mance Building
Ottawa, ON K1A 0K9
Paul F. Cochrane, Assistant Deputy
Minister (613) 957-7701
Dr. Gillian I. Lynch, Director
General, Occupational and
Environmental Health Services
Directorate (613) 957-7669
Paul Glover, Director General, First
Nations and Inuit Health Programs
(613) 952-9616
Dr. Jay A. Wortman, Director
General, Non-Insured Health
Benefits Directorate (613) 954-8825
Ross Leeder, A/Director General,
Program Policy, Transfer Secretariat
and Planning (613) 957-3402

Pest Management Regulatory Agency
2250 Riverside Drive
Ottawa, ON K1A 0K9
Dr. Claire Franklin, Executive
Director (613) 736-3708

Parent-Teacher Conferences

Communicating with each student's parents is one of the most important tasks you will do as a teacher. A link between the student's family and the classroom is critical in helping the student develop his or her skills to the fullest. Each elementary and secondary school arranges parent-teacher conferences for all students. During these conferences, you share the student's academic and social strengths and weaknesses with the parent(s), who, in turn, provide insights into the student's development and background. As teachers, we need to carefully plan for these formally arranged parent-teacher conferences. Here are some suggestions.

1. Try to make the parents feel comfortable. Remember that coming to school to talk to a teacher is not a daily habit for parents. Some may have had unpleasant school experiences themselves. It is your responsibility to put the parent at ease. Suggest that your school provide coffee or juice and cookies for those parents who arrive early, or offer it yourself.

2. Begin *and* end the conference on a positive note. Beginning on a positive note will help the parent(s) feel more relaxed and less defensive about their child. Ending on a positive note makes them feel good about their child, themselves, and you as their child's teacher.

3. Share with parents positive attributes that you have observed in their child. For a few students, it may be difficult to readily point out a positive quality, but if you try, you will find one. The trait may or may not be academic, such as knowing all the multiplication tables up to eight or being able to write a biography. It could pertain to work habits, such as always handing in homework on time (even if the homework is done wrong most of the time, the student does do it!), arriving on time for class, or being honest in saying he or she doesn't understand something. Whatever it is, point it out at the beginning of the conference.

4. Maintain a professional composure and manner, including confidentiality. Don't talk about other students. If parents want to talk about another student, change the direction of discussion and bring it back to their child.

    Don't second guess other teachers, school administrators, or the school board in front of parents. You may not fully agree with your colleagues, but you should never demonstrate unprofessional behavior by questioning their views or decisions with parents.

    Make certain that other parents cannot overhear your discussion with another set of parents about another student.

5. Remember that the parent should dominate the discussion. After all, these meetings are "parent-teacher" conferences, not "teacher-parent" conferences. You need to open the discussion, present evidence of the student's work, and, most important, be a good listener. Answer the parents' questions directly. Avoid educational jargon, and use language that parents can readily understand.

6. Above all, be honest. Don't paint a picture of an outstanding student when the child isn't. Don't be overly critical either. Being a parent is a very difficult job.

Keeping these suggestions in mind, review the following examples of ways to think about parent-teacher conferences in three different situations—early childhood, middle school, and special education. Some of these can be adopted for secondary parent-teacher conferences as well.

Early Childhood Conference Model

The following model was designed to assist teachers in the process of interacting with parents, particularly in scheduled meetings. Although all conferences are different and there are no set answers, the model provides ideas to help teachers communicate effectively and establish partnerships with parents.

When meeting with parents, time is limited and in some cases both teacher and parent may be nervous and/or uncomfortable. The following guidelines may enable teachers to better prepare and work through problems in conferencing. To date, there are no models from which teachers can learn conferencing skills. This model is based on the literature concerning conferencing techniques and research on effective conferencing. Lawler's previous teaching experience has also contributed significantly to the design.

The Lawler Model*

L—*LOCATE* records, materials, etc., necessary for effectively interacting with parents.

A—*ARRANGE* the environment for a relaxed, pleasant atmosphere.

W—*WORK* toward "partnerships" with parents. (Do *not* dominate the conference!)

L—*LISTEN* more than 50 percent of the planned conference time.

E—*EVALUATE* the conference as it proceeds.

R—*RESPOND* to the parents in terms of follow-up.

L—*Locate* **records, materials, etc., necessary for effectively interacting with parents.**

1. Plan an agenda, selecting two to four priority goals for each child (5).
2. Send the agenda to parents with a note requesting time preferences for the conference.
3. Ask the parents if they have concerns to discuss (5).

A—*Arrange* **the environment for a relaxed, pleasant atmosphere.**

4. Arrange the environment so that parents will feel comfortable. The room should be neat and orderly. Examples of children's work should be displayed attractively. Show the parents where their child sits, works, etc. (*Note:* Providing a small table and chair outside the classroom also supports the idea of comfort for parents who have to wait.)
5. Have adult-sized chairs in which the parents and you may sit.
6. Greet each parent at the door using *your* first name. Clarify parents' names with your records. Many children are from divorced, blended, and stepparent families today. All family members are not addressed by the same last name.
7. Sit beside or at an angle from the parent. *Never* sit behind your desk or at a table across from the parent. It is intimidating.

*The Lawler Model, published in Lawler, 1991, *Parent-Teacher Conferencing in Early Childhood Education*. Washington DC: NEA. Reprinted by permission of the author.

W—*Work* toward partnerships with parents (do not dominate the conference).

8. Begin on a positive note. Think of something good to say about each child. (If you cannot think of anything positive to say about a particular child, ask colleagues for help. Be sure to begin on a positive note.)

9. Keep a notepad nearby and take notes. You cannot remember the suggestions/recommendations of all parents. Parents should also see that their input is important enough for you to record and utilize. (*Note:* If parents object to your writing comments, assure them it is for your benefit only, that conference discussions are confidential.)

10. Discuss educational plans and concerns.

11. Be clear and concise. Do not use jargon. (Even the names of tests—for example, MAT-6 [Metropolitan Achievement Test, Version 6]—should be explained.)

12. Do not talk down to parents. If you practice in front of a mirror and your eyebrows are never in a relaxed position, but are always raised, this is a sure sign that you are, indeed, talking in a condescending manner.

13. Base judgments on available *facts* from actual situations. Never repeat comments of other teachers or students to parents. Document behavior when discussing incidents. No one can be expected to relate detailed information concerning all students to all parents. Keep records.

14. Be constructive in all suggestions to parents (26). We know that parents consider their children extensions of themselves. When a teacher is criticizing the child, parents also feel criticized. Parents may often feel intimidated by teachers, regarding knowledge of parenting skills (or lack thereof). Teachers are the experts in the eyes of parents (generally). Be careful.

15. Offer more than one solution to a problem. Treat parents as adults by providing alternatives so that they may have specific input and feel that they contribute.

L—*Listen* more than 50 percent of the planned conference time. The information gained *from* the parent is equally as important as the information you have to share.

16. Talk less than 50 percent of the scheduled time. You are a facilitator, not a director or dictator.

17. Listen carefully and paraphrase for clarification. If parents are intimidated and/or nervous, they may not express themselves well. While hearing back the message you received, they may realize that it was not the one they meant to send. Give them support and assistance in this interactive process through paraphrasing.

E—*Evaluate* the conference as it proceeds.

18. Make necessary adjustments in the agenda while conferencing.

19. Mentally ask yourself how the conference is proceeding.

20. Ask for and accept suggestions from parents. Some teachers are often afraid of what they might hear. Be open-minded and willing to listen and respond to parental suggestions. Remember, the parent has known the child much longer than you have known the child.

R—*Respond* to the parent in terms of follow-up.

21. Make *educational plans* for future accomplishment of goals and objectives. If parents are to become partners, they must be included in some way by making follow-up arrangements. When a conference ends and the parent is "dismissed" by the teacher, the parent often feels as if he/she is no longer needed and has no further part to play in the educational process. Parents come to school from many walks of life and, as in working with children, teachers must work with them on their levels. A single conference during the school year is not enough to develop a partnership with the parent.

22. Allow for parental input in *all* aspects of the child's education. Always make educational plans with the parents to *respond* to their needs and those of the child.

23. Summarize the key points of the conference.

24. Plan for follow-up communication. (This item is often omitted, but it is most important.) Never end a conference without planning what type of future interaction will occur between you and the parent. Follow-up may consist of a note sent home, a note from the parent, a phone call, or (ideally) a face-to-face conference.

The Parent-Teacher Conference in the Middle School*

Parent interest in schools has never been greater than at present. Parents expect full information about school programs and particularly information about the progress of their children. They are entitled to it. The parent-teacher conference is an important vehicle for communication. It provides for a two-way exchange of information about the student. It may be used as a supplement to the report card, but, because it can do much more than a report card alone, it is increasingly being used. However, to make the best use of this technique requires careful planning on the part of middle school staff. In some schools, the student also participates in the conference, making it a three-way exchange of information.

What Parents Want to Know

1. What subjects the students will study—the curriculum for the year.
2. An explanation of the grading system and how it works.
3. How much emphasis is placed on the basics and on other studies.
4. Pertinent school policies, school rules, and procedures, including discipline.
5. How parents can help students learn.
6. Homework policies.
7. What you, the teacher, expect of the student.
8. How well students get along with others (i.e., are they well liked)?

What Teachers Can Learn from the Conference

1. Information about how the student is treated at home.
2. How the student feels about school, teacher, and other students as reported by parents.
3. Strengths or interests the student has that may not have shown up in school.
4. Any problems regarding homework or study habits that show up at home.

Tips for Better Parent-Teacher Conferences

1. Prepare for the conference! Make an outline covering major points you want to discuss. You might want to send a copy of this brief outline of topics home to parents after they have confirmed the parent-teacher conference date and time. Stick to the outline!
2. Be courteous and cheerful.
3. Give the parents a chance to talk first and to share their views and their problems.
4. Be a good listener.
5. Be truthful but tactful. Don't forget that a child is a most precious possession!

*From Louis G. Romano and Nicholas P. Georgiady, *Building an Effective Middle School*. Copyright © 1994 Wm. C. Brown Communications, Inc., Dubuque, Iowa. Reprinted by permission of Times Mirror Higher Education Group, Inc., Dubuque, Iowa. All Rights Reserved.

6. Try to avoid prescribing solutions. Offer suggestions and alternatives. Give parents a part in deciding any action to be taken.

7. Begin and end on a positive note.

The value the parent-teacher conference can have is quite apparent when one examines the lists of expectations held by parents and teachers. Both parents and teachers learn more about each student. Teachers learn how the child is treated at home and what bearing, if any, this may have on behavior in school. Parents can learn about the year's work for students, what is expected of students, how the teacher and the school function, and most importantly, that teacher and school are there to help in every way possible. Besides direct benefits for learning by students, the parent-teacher conference has great public relations potential that cannot be overlooked.

Parent-Teacher Conferences for Exceptional Children*

Be aware of some basic do's and don'ts of parent-educator relationship building. Although lists seldom provide a comprehensive statement of desired outcomes, they can serve to remind individuals of certain basic elements that need to be considered. This also applies to the creation of trust between parents and educators.

Do's

1. Maintain a sense of humor.
2. Be accepting of yourself and the parents and family members with whom you work.
3. Demonstrate warmth and sensitivity.
4. Be positive.
5. Demonstrate respect for the parents and families with whom you work.
6. Be sincere.
7. Listen.
8. Use language that parents and family members can understand.
9. Attend to the emotions and body language of parents and family members.
10. Reinforce parents when it is appropriate.

Don'ts

1. Don't attempt to be a sage who has all the answers.
2. Don't make premature judgments.
3. Don't be overly critical.
4. Don't threaten, ridicule, or blame parents and families.
5. Avoid arguing with parents and family members.
6. Avoid strong expressions of surprise and concern.
7. Avoid making promises and agreements that you may not be able to keep.
8. Don't patronize parents and family members.
9. Avoid making moralistic judgments.
10. Don't minimize what parents and family members have to say about their child.

*Simpson, R. L., *Conferencing Parents of Exceptional Children*, 2d ed. Copyright © 1990 Austin, Texas: Pro-Ed: 146–7; 266–7.

Preconference Planning

The success of the parent-educator progress report conference will be highly correlated with preconference planning efforts (Barsch 1969; Ehly, Conoley, and Rosenthal 1985). These planning efforts should involve attention to the following:

- The child's records, including the IEP [individualized education program] and previous parent-educator conference notes, should be reviewed carefully.
- An outline of those items to be discussed should be prepared.
- The conferencer should review standardized test data that may need to be reinterpreted to the parents and family members.
- A careful selection of papers and work samples should be made in preparation for the conference. These samples should be representative and illustrative of particular concepts and should be dated and sequentially arranged for comparative purposes.
- Parents should be provided a folder of their child's work to take with them after the conference. This work sample should be representative of their child's performance and consistent with feedback provided by the conferencer. Evaluative comments should be provided on the papers to aid parents and family members in understanding the concepts being illustrated.
- Educators should plan for an acceptable environment for the session. This should include a professional and confidential setting. In addition, the conferencer should make arrangements for adult-size furniture for all participants and pad and pencil for note taking.
- Parents and family members should be prepared to participate in the conference.
- The educator should prepare each child for the conference. This will basically consist of apprising the child of the purpose and nature of the session to be conducted with the parents and the materials to be reviewed. The pupil should be offered an opportunity for input into the agenda. Finally, it is recommended that participation of the pupil in the session be considered. In instances in which such participation is appropriate, the pupil should be provided training (e.g., information, discussion opportunities, and role playing) in participating in the conference. These preliminary efforts can aid in reducing the anxiety of both the pupil and the parents.

Off the Shelf

The following list includes books from the self-help section of many libraries and bookstores. These books address areas that you or your students may need help with. This is not an exhaustive list but will give you an idea of what is available. The books are listed alphabetically by title. Check the author's credentials when looking for resources, and remember that self-help books cannot replace mental (or physical) health professionals.

Body Traps by Judith Rodin. William Morrow.

The Boys & Girls Book About Divorce by Richard Gardner. Jason Aronson.

Conversationally Speaking by Alan Garner. Lowell House Extension Press.

Coping with Difficult People by Robert Bramson. Dell Publishing.

Coping Skills Interventions for Children and Adolescents by Susan G. Forman. Jossey-Bass Publishers.

Drama of the Gifted Child by Alice Miller. Harper Collins.

Frames of Mind: The Theory of Multiple Intelligences by Howard Gardner. Harper Collins.

How to Get Control of Your Time and Your Life by Alan Lakein. Signet.

How to Save the Children by Amy Hatkoff and Karen Kelly Klopp. Simon & Schuster.

The Ideal Problem Solver by Bransford Stein. W.H. Freeman and Company.

Magic of Conflict by T. Crum. Simon & Schuster.

The New York Times Parents' Guide to the Best Books for Children by Eden Lipson. Random House.

Organize Yourself by Ronni Eisenberg. Macmillan.

Organizing for the Creative Person by Dorothy Lehmkohl and Dolores Cotter Lamping. Crown Publishers.

People Skills by Robert Bolton. Touchstone.

The Relaxation and Stress Reduction Workbook by Martha Davis, Elizabeth Eshelman, and Matthew McKay. New Harbinger.

The Seven Habits of Highly Effective People by Stephen R. Covey. Simon & Schuster.

Shyness by Philip G. Zimbaro. Addison Wesley.

Speaking Your Mind in 101 Difficult Situations by Don Gabor. Simon & Schuster.

Stress Management by Edward A. Charlesworth and Ronald G. Nathan. Ballantine.

The Stress Solution by Lyle Miller and Alma Dell Smith. Pocket Books.

To Listen to a Child by T. Berry Brazelton. Addison Wesley.

Understanding Culture's Influence on Behavior by Richard Brislin. Harcourt Brace Jovanovich.

What to Say When You Talk to Yourself by Shad Helmstetter. Pocket Books.

The Job Search Process

Begin Your Preparation Early

The fall market can begin the previous November for college/university and in March for public school jobs. *Be flexible* regarding location, levels you will teach, school size, etc.; know what you want, but be willing to adjust to the reality of the market. ***Keep a record* of all your job-search activities,** so you will know what has been done and what you still need to do.

1. *Assess yourself and your goals.* What do you want to teach and where? Do you have personal preferences or limitations, and what alternatives have you or will you consider? What are your strengths and weaknesses?

2. *Locate job information sources,* and evaluate the market in your field(s). Use the placement office, your department faculty, friends, colleagues in the field, and professional associations and/or journals and other publications. Stay up-to-date on job search techniques.

3. *Prepare/collect the necessary materials* for your job search, and make sure everything is current and will be available when needed:
   - EMPLOYMENT CREDENTIAL, including references, to be sent by your placement office.
   - RÉSUMÉ, to copy and send with letters and to take to interviews.
   - LETTERS—of application; of inquiry to a specific school or location; of follow-up to indicate continued interest; of thank-you for interviews—do samples to follow later.
   - PERSONAL FILE—copies of résumé; transcripts; lesson plans and special programs developed; personal references and other evaluations not in your credential; photos; tapes; slides; performance programs; exhibit lists; publications lists; personal statement; etc.—to send when requested and to take to interviews.

4. *Apply for jobs,* when you hear of an opening, by sending an application letter and your résumé. Write inquiry letters and send a résumé to specific areas in which you are interested. If and when the employer so requests, also send materials from your personal file, ask your placement office to send credentials, and have the transcript office send a copy of your transcript. Late in the year, or when there are close deadlines, you may want to phone the employer to find out what you can do to speed up the process and to encourage an interview.

Source: Educational Placement & Career Services, University of Wisconsin–Madison, Madison, Wisconsin. Reprinted by permission.

5. *Prepare for interviews;* plan what questions you will ask, and find out what employers are looking for and what questions can typically be expected from them. Use libraries, chambers of commerce, colleagues, and the placement office to research schools and communities.

6. *Follow up* on applications periodically; do not wait to be contacted. Send thank-you letters for interviews, and follow up if you are not contacted by an agreed-upon date. Remain *active* in your job search—be assertive! REMEMBER that you are responsible for finding your job.

Typical Interview Questions (K–12)

For the Teacher Candidate

In preparing yourself for the employment interview, consider kinds of questions that the interviewer may ask you. Most interviewers ask questions that fall into four major categories: (1) personal qualifications and background, (2) interpersonal relationships, (3) the teaching-learning process, and (4) professional qualifications and experience. The following questions are representative of those that might be posed in each of the four categories:

A. *Personal Qualifications and Background*

1. Why do you want to teach?
2. What gives you the most satisfaction as a teacher?
3. What can you contribute to our school?
4. Tell me about your personal background.
5. What are your hobbies and interests?
6. What would you like to be doing professionally five years from now?
7. Why do you think you will be a successful teacher?
8. Why should I hire you instead of other applicants?
9. What extra-duty activities would you be willing to assist with?
10. What are your strongest traits? Your weakest trait(s)?

B. *Interpersonal Relationships*

1. What quality in other people is most important to you?
2. Would you enjoy team-teaching?
3. What do you believe your role and obligations to be toward other faculty members?
4. What techniques do you use in developing rapport with students?
5. How do your students react to your teaching?
6. What are the qualities of some of the best teachers you have studied under or worked with?
7. How do you feel you relate with minority students in the classroom?
8. What do you see your relationship to be with the parents of the students in your classroom?

Source: Educational Placement & Career Services, University of Wisconsin–Madison, Madison, Wisconsin. Reprinted by permission.

9. How would you work with students in your classroom who are handicapped or disadvantaged in some way?

10. What procedures work best for you in maintaining discipline?

C. *The Teaching-Learning Process*

1. How do you handle curricular content in classes with many levels of ability?

2. How would you individualize instruction in your classroom?

3. What do you consider to be the most worthwhile innovations in your particular field(s)?

4. Describe the role of the teacher in the learning process.

5. What do you consider to be an ideal learning environment?

6. How would you organize and what would you include in a unit lesson plan?

7. What "pet" ideas or innovations do you plan to use in your teaching?

8. How do you expect to motivate students?

9. What do you think of the letter grade system?

10. What would you do or how would you treat a student who refused to do the work assigned?

D. *Professional Qualifications and Experience*

1. Why did you choose your particular area of preparation?

2. What have you learned from your student teaching experience?

3. What grade level do you feel most competent teaching? Why?

4. What out-of-school experiences have you had working with children?

5. What kinds of work experience have you had other than teaching?

6. What courses do you feel competent to teach?

7. How effective has your university been in preparing you for teaching?

8. What is the purpose or place of your subject on the school curriculum?

9. How do you define education?

10. What would you do if . . . ? (hypothetical situations regarding curriculum, methods, texts, student relationships, professionalism, and discipline)

For the Employer

You will want to be prepared to obtain information as well as give it, so if the employer does not cover everything you want to know, do not hesitate to ask about the following and anything else you may have questions on:

A. *The Teaching Assignment*

1. Specific information concerning classload and subjects to be taught

2. Extra-class assignments

3. Physical facilities

4. Available equipment/teaching aids

5. Texts

6. Other responsibilities

B. *Information About the School*

1. Educational philosophy, programs, future plans

2. The school curriculum

3. Availability of study guides and special supervisory help

4. Length of school periods, school day, and school year
5. Number of teachers in system
6. Personnel data concerning staff, that is, average age, number of years of experience, etc.
7. Student data, teacher-pupil ratio
8. Nature and condition of physical plant
9. Special classes/mainstreaming
10. Record and grading system
11. Enrollment trends

C. *Information About the Community*
1. Location and population of community
2. Transportation facilities
3. Educational and cultural background of community
4. Tax base or financial ability of community to support schools
5. Recreational opportunities
6. Churches available
7. Nature of vocational groups
8. Civic activities and vigor of community

D. *Personal Information*
1. Availability and cost of housing
2. General cost of living
3. Salary details and nature of "fringe" benefits

Letters
of Inquiry

The purpose of the letter of inquiry is to introduce yourself to an employer and to inquire if a vacancy exists or is anticipated in the fields for which you are qualified. You write a letter of inquiry when you are interested in a specific school or location and want to know about the availability of jobs there. It is not an application for a specific position, but rather an inquiry about possible openings, whether full-time, part-time or substitute. Whenever possible, address the letter to a particular individual (e.g., personnel officer, district administrator, principal, department chairperson). Names of appropriate individuals can be found in directories available in your placement office or in the reference room of some libraries.

The *opening paragraph* of a letter of inquiry should state why you are writing to the employer and the type of position you are seeking. You may also want to include a sentence or two on why you want to live or teach in the employer's area.

The *middle paragraph(s)* should include information on your qualifications in your field, based on your education and past experiences. Mention where and when you received your latest college degree, as well as your major and minor teaching fields. It may be helpful to include extracurricular interests like coaching to enhance your background. Since you will be enclosing a *résumé* with your letter of inquiry, don't repeat everything from it in your letter; rather, limit your comments to highlights of your résumé, emphasizing special skills or experiences.

The *concluding paragraph* should indicate the name and address of the placement office where your employment credential is on file, and information on how you can be contacted. In closing, you will also want to request application forms and/or information about the school district. One page should be ample for the inquiry letter.

It is time consuming to write letters of inquiry, but the time spent will hopefully result in your obtaining a teaching position. A typed (or even handwritten) letter is preferable to letters that have been copied by machine. This letter provides a first impression of you, and first impressions are important, whether in a letter of inquiry or the first few minutes of a job interview.

Responses to letters of inquiry vary. Some schools, especially those with a small clerical staff, may ignore your letter unless a legitimate vacancy exists. Enclosing a stamped, self-addressed envelope may encourage a response. Other districts may send you a postcard indicating they have no openings in your field, but that they will keep your résumé on file in case an opening does occur. Some schools will automatically send you an application form and perhaps some information on their district. This does not necessarily mean that they have a vacancy, but you will need to complete the application form to be considered for a position if one does open.

Source: Educational Placement & Career Services, University of Wisconsin–Madison, Madison, Wisconsin. Reprinted by permission.

Consider the best time to send letters of inquiry. Elementary and secondary schools generally begin their search for teachers in the spring. Letters sent too early might be ignored, while those sent in March, April, and May will probably get the most response. You may need to send letters in the spring, *and* again in late June or July, to maintain contact with those districts that have at least acknowledged your first letter. By showing continued interest in a school district, you will enhance your chances of being considered as a prospective candidate when vacancies arise. Keep a record of the schools to which you have written, as well as the responses they have made to your letters of inquiry, so you will know which schools need to be contacted again.

The Letter of Application

A letter of application is written to a prospective employer when you know an opening for which you are qualified actually exists. The letter will provide the employer with a first impression of you, including your ability to communicate, so it is important to construct the letter carefully and type it neatly on good-quality stationery. Check for spelling, punctuation, and grammatical errors. Address your letter to the individual whose name is given in the vacancy listing, and include a copy of your résumé with the letter of application.

Since you have some information about the position (e.g., tenth-grade English and advisor to the school yearbook), the letter of application can and should be more specifically written than a letter of inquiry. You will want to highlight information from your résumé that relates to the position (e.g., that you student taught at the tenth-grade level, that you have several credits in journalism, or that you were the editor of your high school annual).

The *opening paragraph* typically states why you are writing to the employer and how you learned of the job vacancy.

Middle paragraphs deal with your qualifications for the position based on your educational background and experiences. You might want to include certification information, particularly if you will be licensed in more than one field. Personal data should be included when it is relevant; an example would be your interest in supervising extracurricular activities. The body of the letter should not be too stiff or formal—let some of your personality come through. A letter that looks like a standard application letter that could have been written by any of a hundred different people will not enhance your employment chances. Another way to personalize the letter would be to gather information about the school so that you can identify ways in which you would be an asset to their program. Although it is not always possible to obtain much information, it can be useful when it is available. Library reference rooms contain copies of college catalogs, and college placement offices often have booklets on school districts which you can review before writing your letter. How much time you have to apply will often affect how much research you can do prior to writing your letter.

In the *final paragraph* you will want to list the address of the placement office where your employment credential is on file and indicate how the employer may contact you. Express an interest in obtaining an interview, and give some indication of when you would be available for an interview.

Upon receiving your application letter and a copy of your résumé, the employer will review them and typically respond in one of the following ways: by merely acknowledging receipt of your materials, asking for more material, sending you an application form, or arranging for an interview. Unfortunately, some employers do not respond at all. This may occur if a large number of individuals apply for a position. If this happens to you, you may want to write a follow-up letter or even phone the employer to see if your letter and résumé arrived and to find out when you can expect to hear from him or her. Keep a record of where you have applied, when you applied, and the response to your application.

Source: Educational Placement & Career Services, University of Wisconsin–Madison, Madison, Wisconsin. Reprinted by permission.

The Résumé

The résumé is a brief account of your educational, personal, and experienctial qualifications for a position. It is used as a general introduction to accompany the letters of application or inquiry you send to potential employers, to promote a job interview. *The completed résumé should be one to two pages long for positions in education.*

As you begin your résumé, review your qualifications for the type of position you are seeking. What is unique about your preparation and background in terms of both your formal and informal experiences and the skills you have acquired? You'll want to emphasize those facets of your experience and preparation that qualify you for the type of position you are seeking. This could mean that you'll need *more than one* résumé, for different types of jobs.

Résumés are structured in different ways. Ideas for format can be found in library reference books and at your placement office, where sample résumé may be available for review. The résumé should be concisely written, orderly in format, and neatly typed. Do a rough draft first to plan the layout and provide for revisions. You may use either short phrases or complete sentences, but try to be consistent in style throughout the résumé. Summarize your experiences, but not so briefly that you omit important information that may distinguish your résumé from the others being reviewed. It may help to ask these questions regarding the information: Does it contribute to my expertise as an educator? And, is it something the employer wants and needs to know?

Listed below are some kinds of information you should include in your résumé, depending on your background. Use the categories and titles that best fit your background. Remember to anticipate your qualifications, that is, include any degree, experience, etc. that you will have by the time you are employed.

1. *Identification*—Your name, present address, and phone number, including zip code and area code, should be listed at the top of the résumé. It is often advisable to list another address and phone number, either permanent or work, where you can be contacted if you can't be reached at your current address. This is particularly important for students, whose addresses often change during the summer when employers will be trying to contact them.

2. *Employment Objective*—This is a statement of the type of job you are pursuing and can serve as a focal point from which the rest of the résumé emanates. It may include your areas of teaching interests and competencies as well as information on the extracurricular activities you are qualified to supervise, research interests, etc. An employment objective tells the employer what you can do for him or her. If you have several possible objectives, you may need different résumés, or you may use your letter of application, instead of your résumé, to indicate your objective.

Source: Educational Placement & Career Services, University of Wisconsin–Madison, Madison, Wisconsin. Reprinted by permission.

3. *Educational Background*—Include information on the schools and colleges you have attended, dates of attendance, and degrees earned, or, if no degree, credits taken. List in order of *most recent first.* Those seeking specialist positions in the public schools will want to include information on their graduate work, both completed and in progress, including area of specialization.

4. *Certificates or Teaching Licenses*—All public school candidates must include information on the fields in which they are licensed to teach or will be eligible to teach by the date of employment. Include the state in which you are licensed, fields, grade levels, and, in Wisconsin, the certification code number(s) for the field(s).

5. *Work Experience*—Employers want to know about your previous work experiences and the *skills* and *responsibilities* those jobs required. Simply listing employment experience is not enough for the résumé. First, prioritize your experiences, with those most relevant to your objective listed first. Indicate the position you held (e.g., English teacher), the employer and location, and the dates. Then *briefly* describe the important aspects (skills, responsibilities) of the experience. If you have a long list of jobs, divide them into separate categories, such as "Teaching Experience," "Volunteer Experience," etc. for clarity. Non-teaching experiences can be included in this section. Be sure to indicate how these experiences have enhanced your teaching abilities.

   For those seeking *teaching* positions, you might include the kinds of courses taught, age level of students, type of school (e.g., open classroom), administrative responsibilities, a unit you developed, a technique you implemented to teach a unit already in place, a description of the learning center you constructed, curriculum development you participated in, and so forth. Stress the contributions you made over and above the expected duties. Student teaching experience, teaching internships, assistantships, and practica should be included and so identified. You may also have non-school work experience, such as summer employment and volunteer experience related to the type of position you are seeking, for example, a camp counselor or tutor experience.

   Those seeking *specialist or administrative* positions may want to include teaching, administrative experiences, special courses taught or developed, etc. Non-school experience may also be listed, especially if it covers a six-month period or longer.

6. *Professional Activities*—A *brief* indication of your activities, such as memberships, research, publications, exhibits, performances, repertoire, presentations, speeches/addresses, workshops, etc., should also be included in the résumé. Memberships might include community and service groups, also, if they are important to the picture you want to present. Each activity can have its own category or be listed with a similar activity if you have only a few entries for each. *If you have a long list of activities in any of these categories, indicate that it is available upon request and put only the most recent/significant entries on your résumé. Keep the list in your personal file to send with the résumé and/or to take to interviews. Remember that the résumé itself should be brief.*

7. *Special Abilities/Interests*—You should emphasize your experience and education in areas that employers find especially valuable, such as coaching, reading education, multi-ethnic education, urban education, etc. Even if you are not aware of a specific need or are unsure of what commitment you want to make to extracurriculars, list your experience on the résumé. A résumé is a tool used to get an interview. A list of extracurriculars may give you the edge in getting the interview. Some individuals may want to create a separate section on the résumé for their coaching experiences and other extracurricular activities.

8. *Honors, Scholarships, and Awards*—Include in this category any college, professional, or community recognitions that are significant to your background. You may need to be specific about the award. Not all employers know, for example, that Phi Eta Sigma is a national freshman honorary fraternity.

9. *References*—It is important to list references who can be specific about your professional competencies or previous employment experiences. Provide a title (e.g., Professor, Cooperating Teacher) and complete address for each reference. Also, list telephone

numbers, since many employers want to speak directly to those listed as references. Remember to obtain permission from those persons you've listed to use their names and telephone numbers.

Remember that employers who read your résumé usually know nothing about you. Have you provided them with enough information to present a clear picture of who you are and what your background has been, yet not so much as to overwhelm them? Have you geared the résumé to the kind of job you want? Does your résumé tell them what makes you different, in terms of interests, skills, preparation, and experience, from the others who will be applying for the same job? Since you are applying for a professional job, did you first present your qualifications and then let the employer see you as a person? A well-done résumé often determines who gets selected for an interview, so it is worth the time spent in careful preparation.

Before you type the final copy, consider having others, such as your placement consultant or someone who has had experience in hiring, read your résumé. They may have helpful suggestions. During the layout of the document, utilize underlining, capital letters, bold print, and white space to highlight key ideas and categories. Be prepared to revise your résumé as your experiences and job interests change. And keep your résumé current and applicable to the kinds of positions you are applying for.

You will need several copies of your résumé, to send to prospective employers. A reputable copy center will reproduce your résumé on higher quality paper so it is clear and readable. Check the phone directory for locations of copy centers. If you wish to have your résumé copied on colored paper or have the layout done by a printer, expect to pay more. Some printers will type and do layout as well as make the copies for you. Remember that although unusual layout, printing, or colored paper may be pluses in producing a high-quality résumé, it is the *content* that matters most.

Job Search Timetable Checklist

This checklist is designed to help graduating students who are seeking teaching positions make the best use of their time as they conduct job searches. We encourage you to use this checklist in conjunction with the services and resources available from your college or university career planning and placement office.

August/September *(12 months prior to employment)*	_____	Attend any applicable orientations/ workshops offered by your college placement office.
	_____	Register with your college placement office and inquire about career services.
	_____	Begin to define career goals by determining the types, sizes and geographic locations of school systems in which you have an interest.
October *(11 months prior to employment)*	_____	Begin to identify references and ask them to prepare letters of recommendation for your credential or placement files.
	_____	See a counselor at your college placement office to discuss your job-search plan.
November *(10 months prior to employment)*	_____	Check to see that you are properly registered at your college placement office.
	_____	Begin developing a résumé and a basic cover letter.
	_____	Begin networking by contacting friends, faculty members, etc., to inform them of your career plans. If possible, give them a copy of your résumé.
December/January *(8–9 months prior to employment)*	_____	Finalize your résumé and make arrangements for it to be reproduced. You may want to get some tips on résumé reproduction from your college placement office.
	_____	Attend any career planning and placement workshops designed for education majors.
	_____	Use the directories available at your college placement office to develop a list of school systems in which you have an interest.
	_____	Contact school systems to request application materials.
	_____	If applying to out-of-state school systems, contact the appropriate State Departments of Education to determine testing requirements.
February *(7 months prior to employment)*	_____	Check the status of your credential or placement file at your college placement office.

(continued on next page)

	_____ Send completed applications to school systems, with a résumé and cover letter.
	_____ Inquire about school systems which will be recruiting at your college placement office, and about the procedures for interviewing with them.

March/April *(5–6 months prior to employment)*	_____ Research school systems with which you will be interviewing.
	_____ Interview on campus and follow up with thank you letters.
	_____ Continue to follow up by phone with school systems of interest.
	_____ Begin monitoring the job vacancy listings available at your college placement office.

May/August *(1–4 months prior to employment)*	_____ Just before graduation, check to be sure you are completely registered with your college placement office, and that your credential or placement file is in good order.
	_____ Maintain communication with your network of contacts.
	_____ Subscribe to your college placement office's job vacancy bulletin.
	_____ Revise your résumé and cover letter if necessary.
	_____ Interview off campus and follow up with thank you letters.
	_____ If relocating away from campus, contact a college placement office in the area to which you are moving and inquire about available services.
	_____ Continue to monitor job vacancy listings and apply when qualified and interested.
	_____ Begin considering job offers. Ask for more time to consider offers, if necessary.
	_____ Accept the best job offer. Inform those associated with your search of your acceptance.